Boys Dreaming

Neil Sheasby

ISBN: 978-0-9565727-8-3

First Published 2019 by
Days like Tomorrow Books

Design by Tony Beesley

Cover design by David Spencer

Printed 2019 by Biddles Books, King's Lynn

For Sonny, Lowell, Mason, Jasmine & Courtenay
Thanks, Love & Gratitude to Claire
Christine & Ray Sheasby

Acknowledgements & Appreciation – Gez Kelly for his editing skills and suggestions, Tony Beesley for making this book a reality and putting it all together, my brother in rhythm throughout this journey Phil Ford, Andy Codling for his Dance Stance archive, Paul Speare for his kind words, Vanessa Beesley, Paul H Snr, Nicolette, Emma, Neil at Chapter Controls, Al Calnan, Nick Read, Peter Playdon, Graham Lentz, Toni Tye, Steven Ellis, all the many wonderful musicians and members of the bands that I've shared these memories with over the years – Thanks for it all...

To Bob,

All the best,

CONTENTS

FOREWORD

I might have been expecting a certain degree of anonymity when I moved from Birmingham to the innocuous village of Polesworth, North Warwickshire – on the modest proceeds of my contribution to the hit single *Come On Eileen* – in 1983. What I didn't account for were two irrepressible teenagers - Neil Sheasby ('Sheas'), and Paul Hanlon ('Hammy') – who were both fanatical devotees of Dexys Midnight Runners and lived just three miles along the leafy B5000 in the market town of Atherstone.

In this book – among many other tales – Neil Sheasby will describe, in his own inimitable way, the means by which he and Hammy tracked me down in those pre-internet days, and sent his dad, Ray, to make overtures to me about producing the first single for their band, Dance Stance. My cover had been blown and I was about to be drawn, inexorably, into their wild and wacky world. As a result, I enjoyed many adventures with them, and in the process, made enduring friendships, which – despite geographical distance now – continue to lead to social and musical collaborations to this day.

What they may never have realised was that they also provided examples, to this sartorially challenged individual, of clothing style which I would subtly adopt along the way!

And now I'm honoured to be asked to write this foreword for Neil's much-awaited book. As years have gone by, I have watched as his interest and skill in writing has developed through social media, generating a considerable following. Neil's vivid descriptions will transport you to places and times, portray characters who you will feel you know, and describe events as if they are happening before you. He will do this with a mixture of irreverent humour, insight, sensitivity and pathos.

You'll laugh, you'll wonder at the incredulity of some of the crazy - but true - episodes he describes, and you'll probably also cry. I never found the anonymity I sought in North Warwickshire, but I gained so much more through getting to know Sheas and Hammy. This is the story of Boys Dreaming Soul.

Paul 'Snaker' Speare (March 2019)

INTRO...

There's a story that my old school friend Noel likes to wheel out about me, where we are sat beside each other in a Geography lesson, and the class is being quizzed on what we are just supposed to have taken in. I of course, have long drifted off, my head in the clouds, totally glazed over and deep in thought. My hand sketches out what my thoughts are pre-occupied with...

As I craft out 'The Jam' logo for the umpteenth time upon my green Geography exercise book, my brain is totally locked into the imagery that Paul Weller's songs conjure up inside my mind. The plight of the man in the corner shop; the grieving mother receiving tragic news of her Little Boy Soldier; the factory worker waiting for the weekend whistle to blow in order to paint on the smell of soap and reclaim his identity; the observational would-be romance where the sunlight flits across her skirt ... it goes on and on, day after day.

"SHEASBY!" suddenly my senses are awoken back to real time. It takes me a moment to readjust to reality

"Yes Sir?"

"Are you planning on joining us today? Have you paid any attention to the question I've just asked you?" I didn't know he'd asked me a question, but I can't admit that now, can I? So I play along with Mr. Gent ... "Yes Sir". Bad move...

"So, what's your answer then, Sheasby?" It would have helped if I knew what the bloody question was, but thankfully for me, my buddy Noel, sitting next to me, has my back covered.

He whispers the answer softly, under his breath. "Oranges".

"ORANGES SIR", I answer with an assured air of authority. Cue fits of laughter from the classroom. No, Oranges isn't the capital City of Uruguay...

It wasn't the first time. In fact, my Weller World school time daydreaming almost set the school ablaze after a Chemistry experiment, where I'd left a naked flame alight around chemicals, while otherwise engaged in fantasising about what to wear for that night's Jam gig at Bingley Hall in Brum. I was quite studious to be fair, but it had to be subjects that I could relate to. English and the written word was cool, even Poetry. Shelley featured on the rear cover of the *Sound Affects* LP, so yep, I'm cool with poetry. Art? Deffo. This is the new Art School ...Weller digs (Pop) Art. Maths? Fuck that! I can spend an hour recreating *The Modern World* album sleeve in biro on the inside of my text book instead. My alternative education was at the altar of Paul Weller, and his interviews were always enlightening. By the time I was fourteen years old, I had read Orwell, Huxley, Oscar Wilde, and become smitten by the works of Colin MacInnes (*City of Spades* is still one of my favourite books to this day). I'd seen Curtis Mayfield, and most tellingly of all I'd formed a band. My path was set. I was already an obsessive. Passionate and spirited, curious and creative, and not even out of school yet. *Dig the New Breed* 'n' all that ...

I thought about my Geography moment just the other night. In keeping with the core of the tale, I ended up drifting off again, deep in thought, my mind wandering. I thought back to my numerous classroom doodles. Days of innocence and anything seemed possible back then. Not wanting to have a reoccurrence of an 'oranges' scenario, I suddenly snapped my train of consciousness back into real time. I opened my eyes. There were people present. Lots of them. Their gaze was fixed in my direction. I found myself in a familiar place, stood to the left-hand side of a stage, my trusty bass felt weightless around my body, it's become like an external piece of clothing (or possibly armour). I feel comfortable, anyway. I quickly re-focus on the important stuff, like being sure to play an 'A' to follow on from the 'G' scale I'm currently working my fingers around. I hear a familiar voice singing a familiar tune. I glance to my immediate right ... no one wakes me from my dream, no one whispers the word 'oranges' under their breath, no one is laughing at me now. This is real, very real...

The figure standing on stage next to me, singing one of our songs to a thousand people, all beaming smiles (and cameras) in our direction ... it's him ... the same figure I used to sketch into my notepads thirty-five years previously. We are now friends; he calls me 'Brother Sheas'. I simply know him as I always did when I drew him. He's Paul Weller. For a fleeting second, I'm fourteen again. I think of Hammy. I glance behind me to the drum kit, and I catch a knowing smile from Phil. Days of innocence intact, and yes ... anything seems possible.

But, as that other song goes ... *How did I get here?*

1- FOOTBALL FANTASIES AND THE SOUND OF MUSIC

I can't get to sleep.

It's not that I'm not tired, I am. I just can't stop looking at the wall. A gigantic image hovers barely a few feet away above my head. While I find it somewhat unnerving, I'm not scared. In fact I find it more fascinating than frightening. I think it's a man, although I'm not entirely sure. The image is alien-like but not threatening, strange, but engrossing and almost hypnotic. I spend most of the night lying awake, transfixed to its every detail. Never do we make eye contact. His eyes are shut, and he has long, dark eyelashes that are seemingly weighed down by the bright red makeup and the mascara that heavily decorates his eyelids. His hair stands tall, brushed back and pulled in at the sides, the length trailing just below his ears, following his neckline. It is flame-red, almost a shocking shade of copper. He appears to be naked, with only his shoulders and the very top of his arms in view. His mouth and lips are very feminine, which is highlighted by what appears to be pink lipstick. The most striking and noticeable feature of all though, is the flash of lightning that runs across his face, travelling over his right eye and the bridge of his nose, a dazzling blood red gloss, outlined in black and powder blue. It's some sight to behold. I finally close my eyes, but I find myself having to keep on re-opening at least one of them, just to check that the freak to the left of me hasn't opened his while I'm attempting to get to sleep. Of course, he can't open his eyes as he's just an image on an enormous poster which hangs on a bedroom wall that belongs to a teenage girl called Leslie, who has the task of babysitting me. My parents are out for the night, and I've been farmed out to stay overnight at the Frost's family home. It's 1973, I'm six years old and my young imagination has just spent the night face to face with the man who sold the world. *Aladdin Sane*. David Bowie. Over the course of the next few months and years, I would become accustomed to the various flamboyant and colourful images of the Thin White Duke. His face, along with other dashing, glamorous pop stars such as Marc Bolan and Bryan Ferry, would appear resplendent and dazzling on the TV screen, while gracing the nation's favourite prime time freak-out, *Top of the Pops*.

Everything just seemed so larger than life during the seventies. Dreams were made in technicolour, virtually anything seemed possible and achievable, and it was a world engrossed in the future. Sci-fi and hi-fi, UFOs, *Doctor Who*, *Star Trek* and *Star Wars*, *Tomorrow's World*, *The Tomorrow People* and *Space 1999*: back then seemed like another lifetime away. It was a wonderful and magical decade to grow up in. Ten-year-olds didn't see industrial strike action, unemployment, refuse waste or power cuts (although I do recall those candle-lit nights being quite fun). No, we were too busy dreaming of becoming the next Johnny Giles or Kevin Keegan, swapping *Panini* stickers on the school playground, playing *Batman* and *Robin*, mastering the moves of Bruce Lee (or even *Hong Kong Phooey* for that matter), becoming indestructible like *Captain Scarlet* or growing bionic limbs like *Steve Austin*.

I arrived on Monday 16th October 1967. The Beatles' *Sgt. Pepper's Lonely Hearts Club Band* topped the album charts, while The Bee Gees held the number one position in the singles listings with *Massachusetts*. I was born in the *George Eliot Hospital* in Nuneaton, although the only reason Nuneaton is on my birth certificate is because this is where the nearest maternity hospital is. My home and heart were, are, and more than likely always will be located in the small market town of Atherstone in Warwickshire. I'm the only child of Ray and Christine Sheasby, who at that time were 36 and 34 years old respectively, and after being together from childhood sweethearts, had probably just about given up hope of having children, until I came along and gave them something that they had always longed for, a son: although my mother maintained that my dad wanted a girl. Apparently, right from the off, I was about to lose one of my nine lives; in fact, I had only been here five minutes and panic ensued. I ceased breathing, and my heart momentarily stopped beating. The midwife became alarmed, knowing I was slipping away. An (off-duty) West-Indian doctor, who was passing the delivery suite, calmly took me under his wing and gave me his full attention until I spluttered, then screamed, and kick-started back to life, ready for this wondrous adventure to begin.

I think my mum and dad felt blessed and thankful, after waiting so long to have children, then immediately witnessing and having to cope with how, with a delicate fragility, life can hang in the balance. I was loved, and indeed felt loved by them, from that day since. I certainly don't believe I was spoilt, or even had the typical 'only-child syndrome'; they just put the time and effort in with me. My dad was especially encouraging, and never put up barriers. It was always a case of "why not?" as opposed to "why?" While I would have liked nothing more than a brother or a sister to share my young adventures with, I didn't really know any different, and subsequently I have always made friends really easily. For a short while, I even had myself an imaginary friend called Simon, though he didn't say much. So, there are no painful childhood memories or nightmare experiences to divulge, no ghost to exorcise. I really couldn't have wished for better parents or a more idyllic childhood. Mostly, I did what all young kids should do. I had fun, and lots of it.

Music seduced me almost immediately. I found its magic and charm irresistible, whether as it filled the kitchen, pouring out of a tiny transistor speaker while my mother cooked Sunday dinner, or as I was sat cross-legged, transfixed to the sound and vision of the TV screen flooding through the living room, my ears always tuned in. My radar was on and I became hooked. My earliest infatuation was with Elvis Presley. His movies always seemed to be showing on TV back then, and I would sit glued to them, noting and memorising his every movement, the shake of the hips, the pumping of the leg, the curl of the lip. He was just so cool; guys wished they were a little more like him and girls just threw themselves at him. Maybe I should get a guitar and hone my own moves? I put one on my Christmas list. Surely, Santa digs Elvis too? And so, on Christmas morning 1972, I excitedly unwrapped a bright red plastic toy guitar, complete with tremolo arm. There was no turning back now. I was just five summers young, and I was in the Rock 'n' Roll business. I started performing the very next day. A Boxing Day matinee show for my mum, dad, grandma and grandad, and the various aunties and uncles who had gathered at our house that day. They all had to sit and watch me mime to *Hound Dog* or *Heartbreak Hotel*, my new red guitar in hand, right-hand side of my lip curled upwards, hips swaying in time to the music, my leg shaking in sync with the beat. Oddly, while I wasn't particularly shy, I didn't have that much self-confidence as a child, but each and every time I got myself lost in the music, I would love nothing more than to dance, sing or mime to records in front of an audience, even if it was only my relatives.

The other music that filled my young head and heart and fuelled my already vivid imagination was that of The Beatles. It is a very weird and odd thing, and I would imagine that I am not alone in saying this, but for me and kids my age it was as if the music of The Beatles had always existed. I appeared to instantly know every word of their songs, like nursery rhymes or hymns. I was born into Beatlemania during the late 60s, so maybe their magical presence had always been lying awake somewhere in my subconscious. It was as if their music had already been installed in our memory banks at birth. Whatever it was, I loved them, and they felt like real people too, tangible and touchable unlike Elvis, who only existed in the movies and my fantasies. The Beatles were a gang. They all played instruments, they wore the same clothes as each other, they sported the same haircuts. If one grew it, they all would, and if one grew a beard or moustache, then they all would. They were a group, a band. They sang about real things, the important stuff like wanting to hold your hand, and being glad because she loves you. Happy songs of yellow submarines and trips down Penny Lane. All you need is love, love is all you need. Ob-La-Di, Ob-La-Da, life goes on, and when you are five years old that is all that matters. John, Paul, George and Ringo. They were like family. I didn't even know that by this time they had split up, and the dream was over. I didn't need to. It didn't matter. I just kept on hearing the music everywhere I went. At home, at school, on the radio, on TV, and most excitingly and intriguingly of all, I would hear their songs played by groups in working men's clubs at weekends.

Mum and Dad both worked hard, and had done so since leaving school at fourteen. My dad was in the quarrying industry, providing tarmac and stone for many major road developments. My mum spent a lot of her life in hosiery factories, making tights and stockings. So, like many working families, come the weekends, they would want to unwind and enjoy an active social life. Usually this meant going to the pub, and as they more often than not had me in tow to look after, they would frequent places that were child friendly, of which back in those days there were plenty. This being due to the numerous working men's and social clubs that provided recreation and entertainment in the form of bingo, darts, dominoes, snooker, food, drink, and not least, live comedy and musical entertainment. We had a few regular haunts. Polesworth WMC was one establishment that our family attended regularly throughout the 70s on a Saturday night. I loved it here; it was here that I would first find myself people-watching. I was curious and interested in the way folk dressed, or the way they danced. Even minor details intrigued me, like the way someone would hold or smoke a cigarette.

The bingo rituals, the meat raffles, the cockle and mussel man in his white coat selling pots by the score from his woven basket. *The Argus* sports paper, or *The Pink*, as everyone called it, due to it being printed on distinctive pink paper. I wondered how it was humanly possible to gather up all that day's football results and reports at 5 o'clock, and have a newspaper printed and delivered, to be on sale at the local WMCs by 7 p.m. *Johnny Schofield's* newsagent's on Long Street would sometimes even have it by 6 o'clock! These were magical social establishments and institutions, where you could witness first-hand, working families painting on the smell of soap, letting their hair down and enjoying their precious time of a weekend.

I felt a real rush of excitement, listening and watching the thrill of a band peddling their craft on a stage, just a few feet away from our table. I think drummers fascinated me at first, but it was certainly the whole experience of hearing a live group that left an enduring impression. The musicians would play the hit songs of the day, plus a few old standards thrown in for good measure. More often than not, the soundtrack to my Saturday night in clubland would consist of tunes such as *Waterloo Sunset*, *Love Grows (Where My Rosemary Goes)*, the anthemic *Hi-Ho Silver Lining*, the novelty sing-a-longs such as *The Banner Man* by Blue Mink and *Chirpy, Chirpy Cheep Cheep*, *Yellow River*, Barry Blue's *Dancing On A Saturday Night*, and mostly all of Tony Orlando and Dawn's big hitters (I always favoured *Candida* over *Knock Three Times*). As more and more ales and *Babychams* were supped, the more bustling the dancefloor would become, which was a sight in itself. It's a funny thing dancing, I suppose, especially watching a load of grown-ups, including your mum and dad, throwing shapes to *Sugar, Sugar* by the Archies or *Build Me Up Buttercup*. Some of them may just as well have had headphones on, as they were dancing so out of time to the beat of the music, but I loved the spectacle of it. Men still danced with women, and together they would throw away the shackles of responsibility, have a shandy too many, get their eyes down for the bingo, and then round the night off by letting their hair down while executing their killer moves to the sound of a dodgy local beat combo churning out all the hits and more. I remember being particularly taken by the mirrored disco ball that would hang from the ceiling of the club. When the stage lights beamed onto it, hundreds of tiny lights would splinter and rotate around the wooden sprung dance floor, and I could easily lose an hour just chasing these little beacons of illumination about.

I would spend a good part of the evenings with other kids, either watching elderly men with greased back DAs and quiffs playing snooker on the enormous twelve-foot tables, or if it was summer (light nights), you would usually hang out by the bowling green, whatever the weather. One thing was always a certainty, and that was the arctic temperature of the toilets in these establishments. It could be eighty degrees outside, but the impact of walking into a working men's club toilet would be like entering Narnia. I tried to get in and out of them as quickly as possible, and I would only really go in emergencies. That wasn't just down to the freezing conditions, though. Being a little lad, it was almost as if the old chaps felt obliged to rub your head as they adjusted themselves and made their exit – "How you doin' young 'un? You enjoying yourself?" Well, I would be if you hadn't just rubbed your piss-drenched, tobacco-stained fingers through my hair! If I ever got tired, my mum would simply put two chairs together, lay me across them, cover me with her coat, and leave me to sleep until they carried me back to the car at the end of the night. And if I did manage to make it through until closing time, I would love nothing more than having the last dance, lodged in between my mum and dad. I'd be hauled about, sandwiched in the middle of my parents, by standing on my dad's feet, balanced on the top of his shoes. This scenario would most often be carried out to the strains of Engelbert Humperdinck singing *I'll have the last waltz with you, two lonely people together...I fell in love with you, the last waltz should last forever.* Or actually, more to the point, it would be a local crooner doing his best impression of Engelbert Humperdinck singing *The Last Waltz*. Magical moments.

There were other establishments we would visit on a regular basis too. *The Miners' Welfare Club* was one in town that would become the venue for legendary teenage discos some years later, but in the early seventies, it always seemed that the "big room" at the rear of the club was only opened at Christmas and for special occasions. I'd sometimes sneak in there with other young accomplices just to run around, and if we were feeling particularly daring, we'd jump up on stage. That would be until the barmaid caught you, gave you a bollocking, and kicked you back out again. I remember that particular lady, as she had a tight blonde perm, and wore a permanent expression and frown that made me wonder if she hadn't had her forehead permed too. *The Legion* in Atherstone's Market Square was another haunt, but usually that would be just me and my dad on a Sunday afternoon. Even then, there would sometimes be a band playing in the function room; pre-Sunday roast entertainment. A few pints then back home for roast beef, Yorkshire pudding, and *Star Soccer* on the TV.

Star Soccer was shown on *ITV* (or was it *ATV* back then?) on Sunday afternoons, and concentrated solely on the fortunes of the football clubs in the Midlands region. Their main commentator was a guy called Hugh Johns, who became best-known for his catchphrase "One – Nothing!" which he often shouted whenever the first goal was scored. Hugh Johns was a bit of a character, and it seemed to me like he had been down the local boozer for a tipple or three before he took to his microphone on match days. *Star Soccer* obviously showed highlights on a Sunday from the previous day's action; you didn't get games being played on a Sunday in those days.

Saturday afternoon only meant one thing in our house, and that was football. My dad adored football! Apparently, he was quite useful as a player back in his day. Some of the old folk still stop me now and tell me of his talent on the pitch, and somewhere I have a photograph of him, pictured as captain of a Warwickshire select team, in front of the *Eiffel Tower* in Paris, while competing in a European competition out there. Unfortunately, his playing days were curtailed a little earlier than he would have wanted, due to a bad leg-break of both his fibula and tibia. That didn't stop his passion for, and involvement in the game though. His team of choice was Coventry City, which I guess is our local side. We are kind of located right in the middle of the Midlands (in fact the centre point of England is situated just a few miles away in Meriden), but Coventry is just about our nearest major city, and that was the club that my dad decided to follow. By the time I was four years old, my dad had become involved with non–league football. He was appointed to the board of directors at *Atherstone Town FC*, and he held this position for a couple of years, along with a good friend of his, Reg Reed. They were faced with the task of steering the club's finances in the right direction. The Adders, as they were known locally, had been promoted from the old Midland Alliance League to the Southern League, where they quickly made progress, gaining promotion to the Premier Division. Dad and Reg made sure that the club adapted to these changes both on and off the pitch, putting them in a secure and stable position. I guess it was like a full-time job in itself, and my dad was by now in a management position at the quarry, so once he had played his part in safeguarding the financial and monetary side of things for the club, I think he felt he had done his job, and he stepped down to enjoy his time off with me, my mum, and of course, Coventry City. The board that inherited this healthy situation ran the club into liquidation by the summer of 1979.

It was here at Sheepy Road, home of the Adders, that I got my first real taste of live football action. We lived within spitting distance of the ground, virtually opposite us on Friary Road. Because of my dad's involvement, I was even allowed to go over on training nights (Tuesdays and Thursdays). The players seemed like superstars to me, and they even had perfect footballer names – Googie Withers, Micky Preston, Smudger Smith, Bob Stockley. A few years later, ex-England and West Brom striker Jeff Astle would grace the red and white stripes of Atherstone Town, and thrilling times could be had on the terraces of Sheepy Road stadium, especially for a young kid with a lively imagination. I found the night games under floodlights particularly exciting. One evening fixture that always springs to mind was one that I didn't actually attend. It was a school night, most probably a Tuesday. This would have been 1976, so I was coming up to my ninth birthday. My dad was no longer involved in an official capacity, but was still quite respected over the road, and when he attended a game, he would often be invited to stay back for a few post-match beverages. On this particular evening, the Adders were hosting Telford United, and I had long been in bed over at home before the final whistle had blown.

My dad, more than likely with me on his mind, decided to invite a couple of the post-match party and entourage over to our house, to sample the contents of his drinks cabinet. Upon arrival, he made his way upstairs to my bedroom and woke me up, which kind of startled me, as it was highly unusual for him to ever wake me in the night. What could be so urgent? Was the house burning down?

"Neil... Neil...wake up, there's someone downstairs I want you to meet ... come on, wake up! You might want to bring your autograph book down too!" So I trundle out of bed and follow him down the stairs, one eye open, one eye still shut, wondering what could possibly be so urgent and important. Who's here? Googie Withers? I kind of just about focused my awakening vision enough as I walk into the living room, only to find *World Cup* winner and England's most famous hat-trick hero Geoff Hurst, sat on our sofa. Ten years previously, he was scoring one of the most iconic goals in the history of world football. Now, a decade later, he finds himself as player-manager at Telford United, and sipping my dad's finest whiskey round our house, with a bleary-eyed young boy in his pyjamas sat at his side, mouth open wide, just gawping up in astonishment. Some things are worth getting out of bed for.

Ray did his best to get his only son to follow his lead and take to supporting the Sky Blues, and I probably would have done if it was not for one fateful day out on Saturday 6th May 1972. Somehow my dad had managed to get two free tickets to that most prestigious spectacle on the footballing calendar (at least it was then) – *The FA Cup Final.* And he took me. It was between the cup-holders and English Division One champions Arsenal, and the rising stars of the era, Leeds United. Now, I have to be totally honest here, I really was too young to remember that much about it. In fact, I can hardly remember anything about the match at all. The only thing I can summon up from that day is the crowds of people, and the sense of occasion. I had never before seen so many people all gathered in one place. And the noise! The noise was just incredible! Deafening! A hundred thousand people all singing, shouting, waving flags and banners. I suppose once again I found myself people-watching. It obviously made a permanent impression anyway.

Leeds United won, thanks to a single headed goal from Allan "Sniffer" Clarke. Their fans cheered the loudest, their players celebrated, they were crowned winners and lifted the trophy on the steps of *Wembley Stadium*. They had the names – Bremner, Lorimer, Giles, Charlton, Gray. They would be my team. What the fuck does a four-year-old know or care about geography? Anyway, over the next forty years or so, I'd become more than accustomed to and familiar with those 106 miles from Atherstone to Yorkshire. You would think, starting with the *FA Cup Final* as your first taste of live professional football, that whatever followed would be an anti-climax, but I really couldn't get enough of it. From the 1973/74 season onwards, once Dad had relinquished his commitment to the Adders, we went to a football match together on a Saturday afternoon virtually every week, until I was deemed responsible enough to travel up to Elland Road with my mates. Responsible? Fuck me, if he only knew what we used to get up to as youths following Leeds about!

For at least a decade, the pattern that our excursions to football matches took was as follows. When Coventry were at home, we would be at Highfield Road watching them. My dad had two season-ticket books, that once again were either freebies, or heavily discounted. I think the idea was that these were secured for his company, *Gee's Quarry*, who were soon to be taken over by *Tarmac Roadstone*, and the intention was supposed to be that my dad would take business associates and potential clients to games, as entertainment and sweeteners to secure future deals for the company. He had the same two seats every game, year upon year, and the only person he ever entertained at that ground was me. He was very friendly with a lot of the staff at Coventry, and I think he had an arrangement with George Curtis, an ex-Coventry captain, who in 1974 became commercial manager at the club. My dad, via his connections in non-League football, would keep his ear to the ground about any up-and-coming talent in the lower divisions, and tip George and some of the backroom coaching staff at Coventry off about certain players. Kirk Stephens, Trevor Peake, Danny Thomas and Bobby Macdonald were all names for whom my dad played some small part in getting them on Coventry City's books. In return, I think the commercial arm turned a blind eye to his choice of what he did with his subsidised season-ticket books. He even had his own parking space for a season or two; he certainly had a way about him my old man. People seemed to like him and respect him everywhere we went. He had a knack of making things happen and getting stuff done, usually without getting his fingers dirty in the process.

On the weekends when Coventry played away from home, and usually the pattern then was one week home, next week away, he would take me (within reason) to see Leeds play. Throughout the 1970s, there was a whole host of Midlands clubs flying high and sitting pretty in the top division of English football – Derby County, Leicester City, Nottingham Forest, Birmingham City, Wolverhampton Wanderers, Stoke City, West Bromwich Albion – so if we weren't at Elland Road on Coventry's away week, then we didn't have to travel too far in order for me to get my fix of the mighty Leeds United. I reckon in the end my dad got the best of both worlds, he was happy that I had got into football, so didn't protest too much when it became obvious that my obsession with Leeds United wasn't going to be just an overnight fad. But he also got to sit with his son and watch his beloved Sky Blues too, and I'm glad we shared our Saturdays together: a father and son bond. Those days were golden, and are ones I will never forget.

It was through my dad's connections and links to football that I first became acquainted with and captivated with circular plastic wax discs.

One of the more laborious tasks that came with the territory of being on the board of directors was to provide match-day announcements and entertainment, which came in the form of just a handful of 45 rpm, 7-inch vinyl singles that my dad would put on repeat at every home game before the match kicked off, again at half time, and also at the end of the game. When I say a handful, I mean just six records. They were *Telegram Sam* by T. Rex, *Indian Reservation* by Don Farndon, *Woodstock* by Matthews' Southern Comfort, *The Witch* by The Rattles, *Patches* by Clarence Carter and *Under my Thumb* by Wayne Gibson. Now, the first observation you would rightly make upon imagining that unlikely mix of audio ambience crackling out of the tannoys on a Saturday afternoon at your town's local football stadium, is that it was more than a little odd. Twenty-two players trotting out to the sound of German beat combo The Rattles screaming out *Can't you see the witch?*, or Don Farndon musing over *Cherokee tribes* was at best faintly bizarre. For reasons best known only to himself, my father used to take these records home with us at the end of every match, and they would preside at our house until the Adders next had a fixture at Sheepy Road.

I made friends with the stereo early on in life. I was fascinated by the stacking of the singles, the drop-down arm, the clicking and whirring, and of course the sound that blared out of the tiny speaker, made by just the slightest needle dropping onto rotating plastic wax. Soon enough, I was allowed to operate the *Dansette*, and I'd play those colourful 45s that nestled in a rack by the gram. Those six singles must have belonged to an elder, semi -hip cousin. No way had my dad been out and bought them; he was more a Ted Heath Big Band sort of fella. I played them over and over. Two stood out for me, and I returned to them much more often than the others. They had a different sound to them - Clarence Carter's story of *Patches*, a sad tale of father and son, with Clarence as the narrator. A pleading, commanding vocal, horns complementing, reaching out, captivating. And then Wayne Gibson with *Under My Thumb*. A direct, stomping, shuffling groove, cool and crisp. I was flabbergasted when years later, I found out that the Rolling Stones had hi-jacked it. I was even more outraged when I discovered that they actually wrote it, and had the cheek to record it before I was even born.

I was captivated by the sound of these songs. I didn't know it then, but I do now, this was my first introduction to soul music.

2- THIS IS THE MODERN WORLD THAT I'VE LEARNT ABOUT

Record shops, always record shops!

It's where the action always gathered pace, a meeting point for kindred spirits. A hive of conversation, connections made, young peacocks showing off and hatching plans. These were the days when platters sold by the lorry-load, sounds mattered, and every tin-pot town in the country had a record dealer. In Atherstone we had three outlets; *Pickerings*, who specialized solely in selling records, but did after a while also incorporate a toy department upstairs, then there was *Woolworths*, and *Lloyds Chemists*, who had a section dedicated to vinyl and cassettes at the back of their store, after you'd negotiated shelves full of paracetamol, hairspray and toothpaste. The girl assistant in *Lloyds* was an amicable sort, and didn't mind us hanging out. To my shame, I once swapped the price sticker on The Who's *Quadrophenia* LP so I could afford it. I feel like I took the piss somewhat and let her down, but I have managed to live without losing too much sleep over it for the past thirty years. *Lloyds* had a cleanliness about it too, the plastic sleeves were always pristine, and you could smell the records as soon as you passed the display of *Scholls* sandals halfway up the shop. I equally enjoyed *Pickerings'* hospitality. Dave, who ran the shop, was knowledgeable, friendly, always willing to turn you on to a new sound or two, and would easily persuade me to convert my paltry pocket money into a couple of new records. I could waste away afternoons in *Pickerings*, just marvelling at the poster displays that not only adorned the walls of the shop, but also its ceiling.

Lloyds Chemists though, held some unusual magic for me, probably because it was an unlikely place to find such an eclectic array of vinyl LPs. I would spend hours in that little space, studying form. I would scrutinize the cover of *Cut* by The Slits, wondering what sound semi-naked women covered in mud could possibly make. I'd be humoured by the sight of a fake plastic dog shit on the rear of the Sex Pistols' compilation *Flogging A Dead Horse*. I'd become curious as to why Ian Dury would call his LP *New Boots And Panties*, and be seduced by the provocative nature of the two somewhat masculine females in their see-through underwear on the cover of Roxy Music's *Country Life*. I'd also hide some of these fascinating artefacts towards the back of the racks, until I had saved up enough money to cease poring quizzically over them and actually buy them, which I did eventually manage to do, with the exception of the Roxy Music LP, which would have felt like I was buying top-shelf porn at the time (I was just thirteen). When my mum and dad went on a shopping excursion and took me with them, I would always seek out the local record shop of whatever town or city we were visiting. Without fail, they always held my interest. They were like old curiosity shops even then, each one individually unique. I also liked the fact you could find record outlets and racks of LPs at the back of an electrical shop, or nestled in the corner of an indoor market, always with treasures just waiting to be unearthed.

I suppose I am what you might describe as something of a hoarder. I don't tend to throw much away, and I guess that I have always been into collecting stuff, even from an early age. I still have a huge collection of *Roy of the Rovers* comics dating back to the early 70s, *Marvel* magazines too, thousands of them, still bagged up, and documenting my young obsession with *Spiderman*, *Daredevil*, *Captain America*, *The Hulk*, *Thor*, *The Fantastic Four*, *The Avengers*, *Iron Man*, and so on. One of my favourite playground rituals was the frenzied card-swapping action during break times, the kids desperate to complete their *Panini* football sticker annuals. "Got, not got, got, got, got, not got!" were familiar daily cries of a middle school lunchtime. I still have all my books (mostly complete), from *Football League* collections through to the glamour of the *Argentina 78 World Cup* book. It's only recently that I begrudgingly decided to part with boxes full of my old *Subbuteo* table soccer teams. I absolutely loved a bit of flick-to-kick action, and I'd still play now if I could find a willing opponent that shared my enthusiasm for a bad back and sore knees; (although the game is officially called table football, I met very few people or kids who actually played it on a table). My childhood penchant and passion for collecting such things must surely have been the foundation and catalyst for my lifelong and enduring relationship with those magical, alluring works of circular plastic art.

Let me just lie down on the couch and I will attempt to explain how all of this began…

We'd always had a few records in the house, and I'd even bought a few myself. The first long-playing record I can remember owning that was mine, and not a hand-me-down, would be Elvis Presley's *40 Greatest Hits*. A double-LP with his face on the sleeve, it was on the *Arcade* label, which was akin to *K-Tel* or *Ronco*, the people that put out cheap compilations. Soon to follow would be records by the Electric Light Orchestra, 10cc and Abba. It was sometime between 1978 and 1979 when I really got hooked. After punk, although I knew very little about that, or what we now refer to as new wave, I started to notice these desirable objects turning up on the school yard, being traded, bought or swapped: seven-inch singles, the best of which were housed in vibrant, imaginative picture sleeves. Excitingly, certain records were no longer bog-standard black either; you had coloured vinyl, some even bright pink or yellow. Certain records were available as picture discs, too; I didn't know whether to celebrate or curse the fact that I was the only person in the school who owned *Cool for Cats* by Squeeze on black vinyl, while everyone else had it on pink, which was obviously far more attractive to the eye. But hey, mine was different! All this excitement transported me back to stacking those six singles onto my dad's *Dansette*, but this was even more intoxicating. I could make my own choices now! This was even more eventful than securing that elusive Mario Kempes *World Cup '78* sticker. This was for keeps. To have and to hold forever. This was the soundtrack of our lives.

Lists started to circulate. For Sale lists, Wanted lists. And then, there was the best of all lists, the Keith Ricketts list. Keith Ricketts was a local punk, a Face on that scene. He was several years older than we were, and it was his list of records for sale that had made its way into my possession, and which I studiously cast my eyes over one lunchtime. I made a note of Keith's phone number, and hastily arranged to meet him after school. I bought as many pieces of that seductive round plastic as my limited budget could stretch to. I was elated at my purchases, and rushed home to play them. I can no longer recall what they were, but they certainly included Devo, 999, The Dead Kennedys, Stiff Little Fingers and quite possibly the Dickies (not banana-yellow, but black vinyl again! Surely a rarity?) But, almost immediately I was taken by one particular record. I became transfixed by its cover, a photograph of the band pictured beneath what looked like a flyover, with two blocks of high-rise flats in the distance. They are all neatly-dressed in sharp button-down shirts. The singer, who is the only one staring directly at the camera, is sporting a jumper with two arrows tacked on to it, pointing in vertically opposite directions. Flip the sleeve over, and it captures the band on stage, black and white suits and ties, sporting matching *Rickenbacke*r guitars, the bass player caught leaping in mid-air pose. The record seemed exciting already, and I hadn't even taken it out of its sleeve yet. It was called *This Is the Modern World* by The Jam. The album was everything I wanted it to be. It still had the energy, drive and anger of punk, but it contained more style and substance. In fact, my favourite two songs from the LP, *I Need You (For Someone)* and *Tonight at Noon*, could almost be described as love songs. I wore the grooves out on it! Little did I know at the time that this would turn out to be their weakest album, or that this same band would soon be responsible for shaping and defining my own musical journey.

It's a golden and magical period, that moment when you first feel the thrust of the teenage kick, when your imagination is captured, ignited and catapulted into an intoxicating world of thrills and excitement, experiencing the adrenaline rushes of life for the very first time. I consider myself very fortunate to be of a certain age. Whether by fate or destiny, my initial sensation for the teenage rush of adventure could not have been timed any better. As the decade turned, and 1979 shifted into 1980, there was never a more perfect moment to become a teenager. Of course, I am sure every generation would beg to differ, but I wouldn't swap my explosion of youthful escapade for anything. 1980 would also be the year that I was faced with the daunting manoeuvre of moving up from middle school to high school. From a big kid on a small playground, to a minnow trying to slip in without attracting too much attention from the older youths full of the tautness of teenage tension; trouble was usually waiting just around the corner. Differences were heightened back then, because youth culture and street culture were both clearly defined. There were no blurred lines, the barriers were set. If you weren't a punk, a skinhead, a rocker, a mod, a rude boy, a ted, a soulie, a new romantic, or didn't adhere to the dress codes of your chosen path, then you were deemed an outcast, a nothing, a stiff, a nobody. I'd become aware of this a few years previously; as I've already told you, people-watching was (and still is) a favourite pastime of mine.

By 1979, a small pocket of older kids started to dress differently. It was a stark contrast to the part-time punk uniforms, all scruffy and cartoon-like, or the tired denim and leather-clad youths that stank of patchouli oil. This look opposed all that. It was neat, sharp, tidy, almost conformist. The cult movie *Quadrophenia*, loosely based on Pete

Townshend's rock opera telling the story of Jimmy, a 60s Mod, was released and doing the rounds that year. In its wake, it sparked a revival and reawakening for a new generation to embrace all things mod, and it quickly spread from cities to towns all over the UK, like a style epidemic. History hasn't been too kind to the modernist revival of 1979, and I can understand and appreciate why. It was a retrospective movement, and went against the grain of everything that the true modernist ethos of the early sixties was all about. But then again, we weren't all born in the 40s were we, or afforded the opportunity to look back through the 1960s with rose-tinted spectacles. Admittedly, some kids did just wear a parka and a button-down *Ben Sherman* like a uniform, and thought they were the Ace Faces of their local youth club disco. Toytown mods, followers, like a herd of sheep, these sorts were not in it for the long haul; they just wanted to fit in and belong to something for a short while. It wasn't about bank holiday beach fights and owning a scooter. For every bunch of kids that didn't quite latch on, and had no desire to become obsessed with the weird and wonderful world of mod and its many different facets, there was always a handful that did embrace the subculture's very essence and ever-evolving nature, and learned some lessons for life.

But for now, we all had to start somewhere, and I began by getting fully-acquainted with my new favourite band, The Jam. I had an older second cousin who was studying at *Leeds University*. He would come home and inform me of bands that he had seen up there – The Police, Joe Jackson, Ian Dury and the Blockheads. I told him of my freshly acquired fixation with The Jam. To my surprise and delight, not only had he heard of them, he had also seen them live already, and furthermore he informed me that they had also released another couple of albums and several great singles. I had some catching up to do. He suggested that if I was serious about keeping tabs on what was happening in the music scene, then I should buy a weekly music paper called *NME*. I quickly did my homework. *In The City,* I loved, but *All Mod Cons* upped the stakes. It changed everything. I spent the next couple of months reading, researching, discovering, investigating and immersing myself in all things mod. I became aware of other bands that adopted the look – Secret Affair, The Chords, the (dreadful) Merton Parkas, but none of them even came close to the sheer brilliance of The Jam, and with *All Mod Cons,* they had found their own sound and were creating their own scene. Punk had burnt out, a whole new movement was about to explode, and The Jam were lighting the fuse. I was now totally up to speed, and for the next release, a new single called *The Eton Rifles*, I could experience the euphoria of walking into *Pickerings* on Long Street and buying it on the day of release. I vividly recall the day *Setting Sons* was released. I impatiently checked to see if *Pickerings* was open at half past eight in the morning on my way to school. Of course they weren't, so I spent all day anxiously anticipating the home-time bell, so I could dash up town and buy it, fearful that they would have sold out already (I needn't have worried, I even got a free badge too).

And so it began, a thirty-plus year love affair. Thousands of kids just like me found their voice. They had something to identify and connect with. I think it's easy to forget just how big The Jam were. The fascinating thing looking back on that time is The Jam's dominance of the pop chart. They were easily the biggest band in the country, and although they attracted an undeniably male following, I remember many girls buying their records too, and putting their pictures up on their bedroom walls, or covering their school notebooks with photos of Weller. For a time, The Jam were the most perfect pop group, and never had that crown sat so awkwardly. The Jam were our band. The Jam gave us inspiration, identity, information, intelligence. The Jam helped me make sense of being a teenager, provided a musical and political education, I would study the inner sleeve of *All Mod Cons* and check the references – *Tamla Motown*, the *Sounds Like Ska* LP, *Biff, Bang, Pow* by The Creation, *the 100 Club*. Doors started to open, and lights went on inside my head. A new (modern) world was already out there waiting to be discovered. Within a few short weeks things started to fall into place. I bought myself Richard Barnes' wonderful book of enlightenment, which was simply called *Mods*. It became my Bible; 128 pages of modernist history to pore over and examine. A couple of those pages featured collages of records and bands that the original mods of the early 60s would have listened to, and I made it my mission to not only hear them, but attempt to collect them. I would start to hassle Dave at *Pickerings* for Eddie Floyd records, or Mose Allison. I gathered almost every title from *Lloyds*' racks that was emblazoned with the *Tamla Motown* label on the rear of its cover. Before too long, my record collection started to expand rapidly, and I would spend every spare penny I could muster on either sounds or clothes. At thirteen I was wearing tonic and mohair; by the time I was fourteen I'd read Robert Tressell, Colin MacInnes, and George Orwell. I had seen Curtis Mayfield and Georgie Fame. Paul Weller and Richard Barnes probably showed me more than most of my secondary school teachers could ever dream of. I seized the moment and dived into this magical world, instantly realising that this would be no overnight fixation or fad. These discoveries were for life. My world would never be the same again.

I thoroughly enjoyed school. The way I looked at it was that I got to spend six hours a day with my mates, play a lot of football and chat a load of girls up. I hated Maths lessons, didn't particularly like Science, but I had a genuine interest in Art and the written subjects, such as English, History and Geography. Those subjects seemed real; they were relevant. I am probably never going to speak Latin, or need to know the square root of 92, but I might want to know where Bologna is one day, or who painted *Guernica*. I was fortunate to drop in with a good crowd too. By birth date alone, it meant that I shared most of my schooling with some great characters, most of whom I remain friends with to this day. Adrian Crookston was my closest associate at school, probably because he shared my enthusiasm for the mod thing. We would innocently spend our Physics lessons sat at the back, singing Secret Affair songs and quoting *Quadrophenia*, rather than learning the magnitude of an electron charge. Even at school, Crooky would juggle his spare time between at least five different part-time jobs, to be able to save up for new threads, or the *Lambretta* scooter that he so desired; he had the bug alright. Other kids would brighten up my day too. Noel Johnston, whose father, Noel Snr., ran the local Atherstone Rangers football side who we all played for. Young Noel was the nearest thing we had to a proper hard case, but he had a heart of gold, and certainly looked out for me on more than one occasion. He kept trouble at bay, especially from any would-be elder bullies who stalked the corridors. He didn't really fully embrace the music thing, but I do remember him turning up once in a full-length military jacket, with a single letter and number stencilled on the back of it – U2 – in fairness he was quick out of the traps with that one, they'd only just released *Boy*. Not many would take the piss out of him anyway. I did of course.

Simon O'Connor was a good 'un too. Like me, he had ideas very early on about forming a band. We probably would have made a good match, but the only trouble was we both turned out to be bass players. Nick Barker was a cool kid, with a genuine Art School vibe about him, and he was always trying to turn me on to stuff; mainly hip indie bands of the day like Joy Division and Eyeless in Gaza. He'd always be in charge of the cassette player in our Friday morning double period of

Art with Mr. Lewis; that's where I first heard The Velvet Underground and The Doors. Then there was Jonty, Jonathon Spokes, the first true eccentric I ever had the good fortune of hanging out with, an oddball from the off, but absolutely hilarious with it too. He was completely double-jointed, and could virtually rearrange his whole body into any shape. We once went away on a school trip to *Honiley Hall*, near Kenilworth, where a few of us would share a dorm. Jonty was in our room, and of course Jonty doesn't do sleep, he's far too wired for such an inconvenience. Instead he decides to keep us entertained by showing us a trick, a trick that I have never seen the likes of since, and to be fair, I probably don't want to either. He proceeds to lie on the bed, take down his trousers and underwear, then arc himself backwards, placing his legs behind his head, wrapping his feet at the back of his neck. This maneuver alone has most of us doubling up with laughter, but what he has in store next just beggars belief. He produces a cigarette, lights it, and inhales on it a couple of times, and then takes it out of his mouth (still with his legs around the back of his neck), and places it in his anus; yes, that's right, he firmly lodges a lit cigarette into the external opening of his rectum. By now, the rest of us, gathered as his captive audience, are caught between having tears rolling down our cheeks and our jaws hitting the floor. Jonty's not finished yet though, here's the trick – once the fag is stabilized in his rear end, he moves his hands away and inhales the cigarette through his arsehole, lighting up the end of the cigarette as if you were smoking it normally. Comedy gold or a horror show? I'm still not sure. I do wonder how he ever found out he could pull off such a stunt! What on earth would make you curious about trying to smoke a fag out of your ringpiece? The last I heard of Jonathon, he was taking up semi-professional wrestling. I just hope he'd got himself a patch and weaned himself off the tobacco. Despite all the many friendships and alliances that I was lucky enough to forge throughout my early school years, I was still on the lookout for a kindred spirit, or a sparring partner to share my vision and aspirations of starting a band and actually begin creating music. As fond as I was of my school mates, I knew I would have to be patient, and look elsewhere.

Punk had been a big deal round our way. Of all the unlikely places for a bona fide scene to blossom and explode was our neighbouring village, Mancetter. At the helm was the aforementioned Keith Ricketts, who formed a band called Bible of Sins. Soon to follow were Hiroshima, Corrupt Youth and Barbed Wire, all of whom had some roots in the

Mancetter punk fraternity of '77. As I rode my pushbike around town, I would sometimes hear these bands rehearsing in local halls or garages. Bible of Sins had the great irony of practicing in St. Mary's Church Hall for a while, until the church found out what their moniker was. The noise drifting from these buildings, escaping out of open windows and onto the street, would make me delirious with excitement. Some of them sounded fucking terrible, but it didn't matter; these were just normal, local youths, Clogger, Strett, Al Ford, Cookie, Daz Storey. Kids not much older than me, forming bands. The DIY instruction of punk rock had taken hold.

The first real friend who I formed any sort of musical bond with was a kid called Nick Thomas. Our parents were acquaintances, and Nick and I had grown up together from infant school, but as we came to move up to high school, both he and his elder brother Chris were sent to be educated at Bablake School in Coventry. Out of school time, I liked to hang out with Nick. He and Chris were the first lads I ever knew who could play musical instruments. They both played guitar, but Chris was also fairly competent on the piano. Nick had some great records at his house, and we had common ground with The Jam, but for a kid so young, he got into some really eclectic stuff. It was in his bedroom that I first heard Essex anarchists Crass, and the spin-off groups from their label, like Poison Girls and Zounds, whose remarkable EP *Can't Cheat Karma* remains a firm favourite of mine to this day. I owe Nick for opening up my ears, and closing down any pre-conceived prejudices that I could have clung on to with regards to listening to music. After all, there are only two types of music – good and bad, and it's up to the listener to decide and differentiate between the two.

The first Adam And The Ants album, *Dirk Wears White Sox*, was a big one for us; that unique imagery caught our eye too, as did its subsequent development. I also remember the first couple of Siouxsie and the Banshees singles being very popular at the Thomas's; we played the track *Christine* until we wore the grooves out. Nick really dug The Stranglers, and especially their album *The Raven*. He had mildly quirky ways about him at times, which I suppose any teenage kid listening to Crass might. One particular day, we're heading into town just to hang out, maybe play some *Space Invaders* in the local café, and Nick decides he's taking *The Raven* LP with him, just to put under his arm and carry around the street as a bit of a pose. We've done a couple of laps of Long Street, and come to rest in *The Corner Caff* on the Market Square. It's here that his Stranglers vinyl attracts the attention of a couple of older kids, who are tucking into their sausage and chips on a nearby table. One of the big kids wants to know if Nick's selling it, and to my surprise Nick says he can have it for a fiver, which in 1980 is a little bit over the odds for an LP, especially for a second-hand copy. But Big Kid has checked in with the local retailers, nothing has taken his fancy, and his sights are set on Nick's *Raven* LP. Big Kid's buying. Nick stalls, says he wants to think about letting it go. Turns out Big Kid and his mate are from Polesworth, and they have a train to catch in less than an hour. Nick strikes an agreement; he's going to consider the offer, and if he decides to sell it, then he will meet Big Kid at the train station in good time before his train leaves.

Three-quarters of an hour later I find myself crouched down in hiding on the other side of Atherstone train station bridge, waiting for the train to Polesworth to arrive on Platform 2. "What the fuck are we hiding from, Nick? There's the kid over there! I thought you were selling him your LP?"

Nick's plotting. "Just wait a minute Sheas, stay down, so they can't see us." Bang on schedule, the train pulls up, and Big Kid and his buddy board the carriages. "Now! Quick!" Nick shouts, as he jumps to his feet and makes a dash for the platform. We leg it across the bridge, down the steps, and to the side of the imminently departing train, just in time to catch Big Kid's attention. He pulls down the carriage window, and seals his transaction with Nick. He pulls out his fiver, which Nick grabs with precision timing, just as the whistle blows and the train chugs slowly into motion. Nick then proceeds to run along the platform alongside the open window, with his Stranglers LP aloft in the air, teasingly just out of Big Kid's reach.

"You fucking wanker! I'll find you, you wanker!" Big Kid's taunts echo back along the tracks as he heads off into the distance, Polesworth-bound, and we flick him the fingers, Nick waving both his Stranglers album and Big Kid's fiver victoriously.

Back at home, the posters on my bedroom wall had undergone an overhaul. Down came *Shoot's* double-page spread of the current Leeds United squad, as did the giant Marvel superhero pull-out poster. They were to be replaced by assorted shots, pin-ups and posters of the Woking Wonders, Weller, Foxton and Buckler. Also a massive movie ad for *Quadrophenia*, with all the film's characters stood along

Brighton sea front, as depicted in the centre of the gatefold sleeve to the soundtrack LP. I had a brilliant *The Who Sell Out* poster, which I'm hoping to find in some cupboard or drawer one day soon, and The Small Faces adorned the wall too. One relic of my childhood which I decided had to stay up was a free poster that I got with Queen's album *Jazz*. It was basically a fold-out photograph of hundreds of naked women riding bicycles. I'm not sure how I got away with putting it up in the first place. I'd only have been eleven when I initially blu-tacked it to the bedroom wall. I suppose you could class it as mildly pornographic; maybe my dad liked to study form when he was pottering around upstairs?

Roy Race of *the Rovers* was eventually discarded as my essential reading of choice, my interests having developed from the affairs of Melchester Rovers to the news, reviews, gossip and gig-guides of the weekly music papers. I religiously bought *NME* and *Melody Maker*, and sometimes I'd buy *Sounds* (until it mutated into a rock and metal paper, subsequently folding) and even teen mag *Smash Hits*, if it featured a group that I liked, which in its early incarnation it often did. I would pore over the pages, learning, discovering, gaining an understanding of all the different offshoots and genres of musical culture, and memorizing names of bands that appealed. Some I latched onto, others I loathed almost instantly. I began to trust certain writers, their tastes seeming more akin to mine, music critics such as Barney Hoskins, Paul Morley and especially Paolo Hewitt, who seemed to have a sympathetic ear for soul, and would once in a while name check the "M" word (mods were often ridiculed in the music press).

It was via the pages of the *NME* that I spotted an advert for a Madness concert that was being held especially for under-16s, a matinee gig, costing only £1 at *Leicester De Montford Hall*. I'd *played One Step Beyond*, their debut LP, to death, along with The Specials' first LP, which I thought was brilliant. A ska revival had emerged virtually on our doorstep in Coventry, via *2-Tone Records*, a label and a vision created by The Specials' keyboard player Jerry Dammers. Releases by The Specials, Madness, The Beat, The Selecter and The Bodysnatchers had sparked a movement that almost fitted hand-in-hand with the mod revival. It was one I would also embrace, and adapt some of its style to develop my own look. While I wasn't keen on the boots, braces and pilot jackets that some skinheads would wear, I did become smitten with the elegance of the Crombie overcoat, tasseled loafers and brogue shoes, and even the emergence of the Harrington jacket, with its distinctive red-checked lining. The rude boys, (who were a different breed to the skinhead), and the mods seemed like allies, and I, rightly or wrongly, would merge the two dress codes. I made my own rules even then and consciously wanted to develop more individuality, and not follow the herd, many of whom just stuck rigorously to the same attire, like a work uniform. The Madness gig was my first experience of a live concert. I went with my older cousin Andy, a lad called Dave Charnell, and another kid whose nickname was, somewhat unfortunately, Emma. I was positioned to the side of stage, on the balcony. Even though it was billed as an under-16s matinee, it was still mayhem, with lads throwing themselves off the balcony and being caught by the throng below, a hall full of skins, rude boys, and mods, all united by the music, which in itself was just exhilarating. It was like *Cup Final* day, but better, a real event. I was left in no doubt. This was the life for me. I was hooked.

3 - YOUNG SOUL REBELS

1980 was a momentous year for me. The most important records in my life were both released that year – Dexys Midnight Runners' debut *Searching For the Young Soul Rebels* and *Sound Affects* by The Jam. If my house was burning down, these are the possessions I would try and rescue. *Sound Affects* was and still is my favourite Jam album. I love its dense, stark atmosphere, its psychedelic overtones. It is a uniquely English-sounding record, which has stood up remarkably well to the test of time. It certainly contains some of Weller's finest compositions. Dexys immediately stood out from the crowd. They refused to fit neatly into any pigeonhole. They distanced themselves from any movement, such as the ska or mod revivals that were happening at that time, and rightly so. They were unique, non-conformist, and they completely blew me away. I loved their gang mentality; they looked different, yet like a team. They didn't play by anyone else's rules or expectations. Even their record sleeves were exciting, complete with essays that would directly communicate with the listener, something they took a step further when Kevin Rowland decided to stop talking to the 'hippie music press' and communicated only via full-page adverts in the pages of those very papers he poured scorn upon. Tales emerged of the group stealing their own master tapes in order to re-negotiate their recording contract with *EMI*. They weren't in the business of fucking about. Dexys were the real deal. And the music! The music was just incredible! If there's been a better debut album, and a more irresistible 3 minutes and 31 seconds than *There, There My Dear* then I've yet to hear it. These two albums, released within the space of a few months of each other, have always been a constant source of inspiration. They were certainly the very reason that I wanted to start a band myself. They were like my religion; I believed, dreamed, cried, rejoiced and existed to the sound of those two records, and their influence, inspiration and importance has not left me since; it is the benchmark I will always return to.

I'd started to get really busy on the record-buying front. I had taken to staying up late at night with a radio by my bedside, so that I could tune into John Peel's show on *Radio One*. I was supposed to be getting some kip in ready for school the next day, but the lure of the radio proved too tempting. I would have to keep it at a low volume so as to not attract any unwanted attention from my parents. I would keep a notepad by my side too, jotting down any stuff that caught my attention. 1980 was a really eventful and quite eclectic year for new music. Punk's novelty factor had worn off, and some brilliant bands were emerging from its aftermath; PiL, The Undertones, XTC, The Pretenders, Elvis Costello, The Teardrop Explodes, Echo And The Bunnymen. British reggae was also coming to the fore, with UB40's debut *Signing Off* and more roots records like the sublime *Bass Culture* album by Linton Kwesi Johnson. I was hearing all this stuff and more, leaping out of the hushed tones of that tiny transistor radio at my bedside. You would have to be patient some nights and bear with Peel's leftfield indulgences at times, but the payoffs were more than worth it. I'd trot off down *Pickerings* every Friday after school with my 'wants' list and purchase as much as I could possibly afford. Music was everywhere; it constantly soundtracked the days. It was important. It was a lifestyle.

In Atherstone, like-minded teens would meet and hang out in cafés, and drink copious amounts of tea. We had a few hangouts to frequent; *Winnie's Café*, *The Corner Caff*, *Sen's Café*, upstairs at *The Roe Boat*, and *The Batch Bar*, which was the first place that had a *Space Invaders* machine. Sometime later, they would be the first to install a sit-down table-top version too. The very day I bought The Jam's *Start* in its garish pink gloss picture-sleeve, I walked into the Batch Bar to the strains of Joe Jackson's *It's Different For Girls*. I sat down, sipping at my tea, while clocking the girl who was feeding coins into the jukebox and making the selections. She was in the year above me at school, and lived in a village just on the brow of the A5 nearby, Baddesley Ensor, which seemed as exotic as Mallorca to me in those days. The kids from there even got a bus to and from school. Her jukebox selection was a double-whammy of *Once In A Lifetime* by the Talking Heads, and then, prompted by the fact that I'd whipped out my 7-inch for her to cast an eye upon, (behave, you know what I mean) she put on *Going Underground.* Our silent courtship was complete. I'd pulled. This amounted to an afternoon stroll in the glorious sunshine down to the Cricket Club, where we had a quick roll around in the long grass, and I got to put my hand up her top and inside her bra (it might actually have been a training vest). After experiencing the dizzy heights of such passion, I got her to pick off the grass that was stuck to the back of my shirt, and proceeded to walk her back to the bus stop to catch the Baddesley Bomber back up the hill in time for tea. We never got to a second date. I think it was her musical choices that seduced me, not her.

Local discos held a great sense of occasion too. Round by us we had *the Miners' Welfare*, *the Legion*, *the Football Club*, and somewhat later *Grendon Disco*, who all held nights aimed at the local teenage community. Youths would gather in separate corners of the rooms in their respective tribes, the denim-and-leather-clad rockers awaiting the metal sounds of AC/DC or Black Sabbath, to which they would perform their preposterous, tired old ritual of headbanging, which I thought looked faintly ridiculous. The skinheads would be in attendance; although in a minority, they still cast an unwanted and threatening shadow over proceedings. "Greasy bastards fuck off!" the hall would unite for that chant, directed at the rockers, and sung in sync with Harry J's boss sound *Liquidator*. You would still get sizeable gatherings of punks, as even in the early 80s they clung on to the remains of the Spirit of '77, especially at the *Miners' Welfare* functions. I didn't mind the punks at all, I quite dug some of the sounds on the quiet, even the more hardcore stuff like Chron Gen, Discharge, The Exploited and UK Subs, plus they were mainly older lads that were into it, and I always got on with most of them; they very rarely caused any trouble. One or two of the young pretenders would try it on once in a while in a vain attempt to gain some standing or respect amongst the locals, but it usually backfired.

I tried my best to stay out of the fights, but my dress codes made me a young target for unwarranted attention, and I had a few unsavory run-ins with one particular group of lads. Their ringleader was a confused sort; one week he was a rocker, the next he was riding about on a scooter, and he didn't take to me at all. A couple of years my senior, he was the archetypical playground bully, although he never troubled me too much at school (maybe due to Noel Johnson's presence). But at the local discos he'd take any opportunity he could find to have a pop at me. One night outside the *Football Club* as I was leaving, he rounded on me with a gang of about ten, who held my arms as the youngest member of his ugly clique repeatedly punched me in the face. I had no way of retaliating, so I took the beating and bided my time. The young pup who had dished out the punches under the main bully's instruction was a youth who was in the year below me at school, so quite obviously I couldn't have that, even if my arms were literally pinned behind my back. Retribution came a couple of weeks later, when I spotted the younger youth through the window of the *Corner Caff*, playing on one of the games machines. I marched in, flanked by Noel and Nick Thomas. He could see my reflection in the screen of the machine. His eyes welled up, but remained fixed to the game. He was alone. I could see his hands start to shake. We all remained silent, until the machine flashed up the signal of the end the game, and I repeated the words on the screen into his ear – "Looks like its game over, youth". It was a market day in town, and loads of shoppers crowded the Market Square, so Noel told him to make his way up the alley that led off Church Street, just opposite the caff. It was out of the way of any attention, just me and him, there'd be no interference from my two mates, we didn't sink to their dirty tactics. I'd no sooner floored the kid in one blow, than I almost felt sorry for him. He was pleading not to be hit again; he was obviously the scapegoat, a fall guy, now crying not to be set upon. He had learnt his lesson though, and in fairness to the lad, he came to apologise on more than one occasion at school that next week, and sensibly distanced himself from the crowd that put him up for all of it in the first place.

It was a few years later, when I had just started tentatively having my first few pints in the pubs of Long Street, that the main bully's grievances with me just breathing the same air as him came to the fore again, but this time I was more than prepared to address his bullying. I was in *The Clock* (actually it's called *The White Bear*, but because of its enormous timepiece that hangs in full view of Atherstone's main road, it's known locally as *The Clock*) on a bustling Friday night, and he decides to attack me from behind, and slam my head into a brick pillar. But this ain't no school playground or kids' disco, this is a busy Friday night on the town, my home town. I'm not standing for another moment of his fucking bullshit, so I offer him outside, and we reconvene in front of a full crowd at the rear of the boozer, by the swimming baths car park, and off we set into each other toe to toe. He's a couple of years older, so for him to get beaten up by a kid who's just started coming out on the pop is something of an embarrassment for him. But buoyed on by the gathering, with whom rocker bully boy was obviously none too popular either, embarrass him I did. After taking a couple of early blows, I eventually caught him with a right that knocked him to the ground; the ring I wore on the index finger of my right hand caught his eye and cut it badly. I seized my opportunity and let him have it, years of his torment unleashed in anger as I rained down punches to his head. I had to be pulled off him in the end, but I had stood my ground and fought my corner, proved that he could no longer intimidate me. I didn't need anyone to stick up for me anymore, or fight my battles. I'd beaten the bully and it felt good. The weird thing about my altercations with both of these characters was that within a year of both scraps, they both died in tragic and unfortunate circumstances. The kid collapsed after inhaling paint thinners, just dropped dead on the spot, and the rocker youth was killed in a motorcycle accident. Despite my differences with both of them, their untimely deaths did sadden and shock me. It was kid's stuff really, and I firmly believe the bully boy would have grown up to be an alright sort, and probably have regretted his unsavory behavior, and me and lad from the year below would have undoubtedly turned out mates; I liked him already. But to lose them both in quick succession, in such a manner, I felt like I was a curse, like the grim fucking reaper or something.

Grendon Disco was a much more sedate affair. It was held on a Thursday night at the local Working Men's Club (yes, those magical establishments again), and the majority of the crowd who attended were all from our school year. Grendon was a short bus ride away from Atherstone, but my best mate Crooky lived on Spon Lane just down the road, so more often than not I'd go back to his house after school for tea and a change of clothes, then onto the disco before my dad picked me up at the end of the night, or I'd get the last bus back to town. It was while walking down Spon Lane one balmy Thursday evening to the club for that night's frivolities, that I had the rather unpleasant experience of being caught short for the first (and up to now thankfully the only) time in my life. I have no idea how it happened; all I know is that one minute me and Crooky are happily chatting away, excited by the prospect of another Thursday night attempting to pull one of the local lovelies, and the next moment I'm stood frozen to the spot with a weight dropped in my tonic trousers. Not cool. Not cool at all. Thank God only Crooky was there to witness it, and he was a good enough friend to me to quickly whisk me back to his house to let me clean up, lend me a pair of his sta-prest for the evening, and keep it to himself. Accidents can happen, and I would have done the same for him. It's only now that he will sometimes shout to me across a crowded pub, after a few light ales "Hey Sheas, remember when you shit yourself walking down to *Grendon Disco!*" Even this embarrassment paled into insignificance compared to the time I got entered into a disco dancing competition to represent the semi-hip mod kids, only to be beaten in the final by a diminutive mentally-challenged minikin I can't remember what his choice of tune was, but he was complete with vest and sweatband tied around his head, while I shuffled around to *Precious* by The Jam, attempting to preserve whatever cool you can while being thrust into some *Saturday Night Fever*-style dance off with a vertically challenged half-wit. He must have got the sympathy vote.

Atherstone is a small market town situated almost in the heart of England, on the A5, or the old Roman road Watling Street, as some still refer to it. It's famed for its hatting industry, which of course is now long defunct. As a man who is seldom seen without sporting some form of head attire, I find it quite ironic that you can no longer buy a hat in Atherstone. In fact some of the natives look at you like you've got something in your hair. How times have changed! I've always found it to be a friendly and welcoming place, with a great community spirit, probably due to the fact there is just one secondary school, and most folk get to know each other right from the off, and form lifetime friendships from an early age. It may also be down to the fact that the town once held the record for having the most pubs within its tiny radius. I cannot deny that the wonderful community camaraderie is often fueled by the town's unquenchable thirst for the drinking culture. Although there have been times when I have been tempted to move away to the lure of the Bright Lights, Big City, Atherstone has always been my home. Its location means I can be either in the North, South, East or West of the country within two hours should I so desire, and the people that I have met here are just the best, not only my peers, but the older generations too. Great characters, quite eccentric also. It's a funny old place.

The only kids who didn't attend high school in Atherstone were the Catholic kids, who would catch the bus to Nuneaton to be schooled at *St. Thomas Moore*. Some Catholic kids, like my mate Shaun Beeson, chose to go to Atherstone, but the majority went to *St. Thomas Moore*. During my escapades around town and at the local discos, I kept bumping into one of the Catholic kids. I kind of knew him, but didn't. He lived on the same estate as I did, just at the back of my mum and dad's house on Tudor Crescent. As kids, we would pass each other on our bikes, and sometimes I'd see him when we played football on the green by his house, though he never really joined in. We were a few years older now, and I'd notice him both around town and at some of the local gatherings, and he certainly noticed me too. He was slight of build, but he stood out from the crowd. Every time I saw him, without exception, he would always be dressed immaculately. It was evident that he shared my passion and enthusiasm for clothes and music, the mod thing. We kind of circled around each other for a while; I think we were both desperate to talk to each other, but like a pair of proud young peacocks, no-one was going to break the ice first, so for a good six months or so we just carried on eyeing each other's threads, and communicated only on the very briefest of nodding terms. He fronted his little parka-clad clique and I mine, barely teenagers, and both of us Faces of our own little gang. It was inevitable that we would fall in with each other sooner or later. It took the foulest of days for our bond to be solidified, fittingly enough in the record department of *Lloyds*, with the rain crashing onto the chemist's windows, the afternoon sky blackened by thunderous dark clouds. I had taken shelter and solace in one of my favourite places. I knew I could while away some time until the storm passed by flicking through the racks of LPs, and it was at this very moment that he swept directly into my life.

Hammy and I. We were an instant mash, a team, a partnership right from the off, a formidable double act. I didn't realize until recently how unique and distinctive our relationship was, and of course I had no need to analyse or reflect on it until years later. He was the archetypical *Boy About Town*, the local Face. Even at a tender age, he had swagger and confidence, but never arrogance. He was brimming with character, and people loved him. We were roughly the same age, though he being my senior by three months put us in different school years, and as I said, we attended different schools anyway, so our paths never really crossed on a daily basis. I was alone that day, he was with a mutual acquaintance Chuddy (Patrick Sheedy), and as the rain persisted, we had nothing else to do but talk. And talk we did. He had got wind that I'd just seen The Jam, and was keen to know all the details. More than anything, it was he who seized the opportunity to quiz me that day. He knew intuitively that I was no 'dedicated follower of fashion', and that even for one so young I wasn't just wearing it well, it was already embedded deep in my soul. It was obvious that we were both obsessives. We talked and talked. Long after the downpour had abated, long after Chuddy had left us to it, long after *Lloyds* locked its doors for the weekend. We walked together down to the corner of Friary Road, and arranged to meet the very next day. I invited him round to my mum and dad's. I remember that Sunday vividly. We played pool, spun lots of records, drank copious amounts of tea, and talked, talked, talked. It was to be the start of forever. We became inseparable from here on in.

Paul Hanlon was the son of Ita and Paul Hanlon (Snr.), his family roots were Irish, and his parents had met and married while living in Birmingham. Paul Snr. was a publican, and Ita had graced many a stage singing for working bands on the pub and club circuit. Their son Paul was born on the 28th July 1967, not long after the family found themselves settled in Atherstone, where Paul Snr. gained employment amongst the local mining community, and Hammy welcomed the arrival of a baby sister, Nicolette. Although Hammy had a perfectly happy childhood, I think it is fair to say that his mum and dad had a fairly turbulent and tempestuous relationship at times. He taught himself the chores and necessity of responsibility from a very early age. I always got the impression that he admired the stability and calming nature of our house; he spent enough time there, that is for sure, and my mum and dad took to him as much as I did, and treated him like one of their own.

We never had time to be bored, and so the "B" word wasn't part of our vocabulary. There couldn't possibly be enough hours in the day to fit all our best laid plans and ideas into. Drinking beer and trying to get served in pubs held no interest to us, instead at weekends we would stay in and utilize my free house, as my parents went out on their social; usually to the *Football Club* across the road. Hammy and I would spend the nights lost in music, discovering and developing our tastes quickly. *Stax*, *Motown*, Otis, James Brown all fought for turntable action with Dexys, The Prisoners, The Small Faces, The Who, The Action and of course The Jam. We got into the habit of dressing up to stay in, dancing, and somewhat bizarrely miming to the records. I had a much-cherished Jam bootleg from *Newcastle City Hall*, which was a particular favourite for us to mime to. Hammy was always Weller, me cast as Foxton. We just about wore the grooves out on that LP, so much so we even knew how long to leave it before coming back out for the encore. We'd fuck off into the kitchen and pretend to have a fag while the crowd (on the LP) went wild and demanded for us to come back on stage for an encore. We were having a particularly good gig (mime) one night, and Newcastle City Hall, aka my mum and dad's living room, was alive with a vibrant atmosphere, our moves even more intense and exaggerated than on previous nights. *Down In The Tube Station At Midnight* was fast approaching an excitable climax, and as the last chord snapped the song to a halt, I leapt up in the air, imaginary *Rickenbacker* bass strapped around my neck, legs tucked up tight behind, a dramatic Foxton-esque jump into the air to punctuate the end of the song … WHAAAM! Mid-air, my forehead made full contact with the living room lights. CRASH! Down they fell on top of me, shattering glass into hundreds of tiny pieces. I remained motionless, in shock for a moment, before looking across the stage (the carpet) to Weller … "Fucking hell Hammy, me mam's gonna kill me!" Thankfully, after a bit of smooth talking from Ray, Christine didn't murder her only son, but Weller and Foxton thought it time to hang up their imaginary guitars and invest in some real ones.

"Let's start a band y'oth", Hammy declared. "My mate Gibby can play the drums, you can play bass, I'm getting a guitar this weekend, and I'll handle the singing too". Hammy had it all mapped out, and I certainly didn't take any encouraging. That very Saturday morning Hammy rang me, excited that he had just acquired his new guitar and amp. We were up and running. I was round at his in a flash. Really, I should have known better. I tried to disguise my initial disappointment as I held the scuffed and battered guitar that his cousin had handed him down only a few hours previously. Even I had to admire the fact that the one string it did have left on it made an impressively fuzzy sound once you plugged it into the barely audible shoe-box sized 10-watt amp that accompanied it. But Hammy being Hammy, he could see past all of these minor deficiencies and viewed it as a piece of gold. The torch paper was lit and we were indeed up and running.

My dad came home from work one day and announced that a colleague was selling a bass guitar. He'd overheard me and Hammy plotting, and knew already that we were hopelessly addicted to music. So, I had been targeted for the bass playing job (Foxton) … "It's got a funny sounding name, Neil … Rick something?"

"*Rickenbacker*? That's what The Jam play! They're the business Dad! Too much money for us though Dad, and I can't even play yet."

A week later he came home from work, up to my bedroom, and handed me the case. I opened it up and there it was, gleaming. A burgundy *Rickenbacker 4001* bass … "You best learn how to play that now son."

Of course, Hammy never pursued his six-string fantasy, not even a one-string wonder. I think it amounted to playing *I'm Free* by The Who on that taut single E string. As far as Hammy was concerned, if he could get one vaguely recognizable riff down, albeit with five of the other strings missing, tick the box, that's the guitar conquered! I thought it best that I should call on a childhood friend of mine who was actually fairly competent, and at least had all six strings intact, and knew the chords to six or seven songs we could play. I called upon my old mucker Nick Thomas, who had already made an effort to start a punk band with me playing drums, which was short-lived. After one disastrous attempt at a rehearsal, it was obvious that even by the limited capabilities required for a punk band, I wasn't cut out for the tub-thumping role.

So, we now had the basic ingredients to start a band. Hammy would sing, Nick play guitar, myself on bass, and Gibby would be our drummer. Gibby was, and still is, a delightful soul to be in the company of, full of conversation, with a sharp wit. The only thing he didn't have was a drum kit, which could be viewed as a slight drawback if you're a drummer in a band. Again, this would only be a minor detail and hiccup in Hammy's book. He would simply shrug off such a small setback with a wave of his hand and say "Don't worry about that Sheas, there's a young kid who lives around the corner from Gibby who's got a full kit we can use". I also learn that the young kid has invited us round to his mum and dad's house to rehearse.

Young Kid is thirteen years old and in the year below me at school. I already know Young Kid as a decent footballer, he has already stepped up a year, and played a game for our side when we were short one time. Young Kid was kind of a shy sort, I'd seen him in the playground clutching a trombone case, but I never knew Young Kid played the drums. Phil Ford lived in Mancetter, on Priory Walk, which did indeed become the house where we first rehearsed, his white drum kit set up in the corner of the living room for Gibby to sit behind. Now Gibby was a competent drummer, steady, and still learning like the rest of us, but he could hold down a beat. However, it soon became apparent that Phil "Young Kid" Ford was a natural. Thirteen years old, he could barely see over the top of the kit, but when he played, it was just magical. It was there and then that I had to make my first tactical switch, put an arm around Hammy first and state the blindingly obvious. "I know we all love Gibby, and he's our mate, but this kid has the drum kit, the rehearsal space, and he can play like a motherfucker. I'll break it to Gibby."

This was a process that would become all too familiar for me over the next thirty years. Gibby, to be fair to him, could see that his number was up, and that recruiting young Phil made perfect sense. We had ourselves a band. Within weeks we had assembled a twenty-minute set that mainly consisted of a couple of Jam songs, the theme tune to Joe 90, and a couple that Nick had written. We called ourselves The In Crowd (we later dropped the "In" to become The Crowd). Our very first gig was in Coventry, at the school Nick attended. We did four songs, supporting more established hopefuls. All I can remember about that night is that I was glued to the spot with fear. I didn't dare lift my gaze from concentrating on what my fingers were supposed to be doing. I was petrified. But once I'd done it, got on that stage, and no-one laughed at us or ridiculed us, (in fact the response was quite the opposite, and very complimentary), I knew I could do it, and from now on, I would embrace it and enjoy it; there was nothing to fear. If I believe in it, then others will too. Our second gig, and first full set, a marathon twenty minutes, was at *Baddesley Youth Club*, a sort of homecoming. We had soundchecked, gone home to get changed, and then arrived back at the gig to be greeted by hundreds (well, about thirty) screaming girls waiting outside. Of course, it was all the birds from our local school, but as far as I know they turned up of their own accord; we certainly hadn't paid them anyway. I looked at Hammy, he looked at me, grins as wide as the sky. This was it. We'd made it. We were somebody. We were the band, The In Crowd. Our hearts raced, our dreams realized on the steps leading into Baddesley Youth Club. Right there and then, in that very moment, we got caught by the buzz, the addiction of an adolescent adrenaline rush. If only Kevin (Rowland) knew, if only more than thirty schoolgirls at that youth club knew. The Young Soul Rebels were alive and well. *Dig The New Breed* indeed! We were up and running!

Now for our own little caper …

3b – Interlude – 1980
MUSIC'S CROWNING GLORY?

I guess it depends on what year you came kicking and screaming into the world that truly instructs an individual's personal perceptions and forms their own information / inspiration and identity. Almost certainly the baby boomers of post-war Britain would declare their teenage kick of witnessing the bona fide birth of rock n' roll as the real cultural revolution, from Tin Pan Alley and Tommy Steele strumming washboards to the sudden explosion of Little Richard's opening cries of "A-wop-bom-a-loo-mop-a-lomp-bom-bom!" – it's very hard to argue against.

That initial burst that connects us to music is the moment we usually spend the rest of our days attempting to recreate, that instant where we become incurables, hopelessly addicted to the thrill of it all, our senses awakened, smitten by finding our very own groove, slaves to the rhythm forevermore....

I myself feel blessed to be of a certain age albeit too young for the onslaught of punk but old enough to have ceased swapping those football stickers in the school playground to pursue a passion that would come to define me. I actually think it is even beyond just collecting music, it's a tribal thing, an awakening. Music at its best far transcends entertainment; it can communicate politics, influence style, inspire hope and confidence, form questions and raise awareness and an opinion. To the obsessive's amongst us these are codes for life, it never leaves you.

Casting an eye over the deluge of remarkable recordings released over the twelve months that made up 1980 it begs the question – has there ever been a better year for music?

Eclectic is now an overused description but that is certainly the turn of phrasing that best encapsulates the broad church that was 1980. Musically, it was a year of experimentation, bold and diverse artistic statement. The fag end remains of punk were all but extinguished, the novelty of diminished and digital technology was yet to get in the way of a great pop song. The year 1980's hand was so strong that even the old guard managed to turn in credible records. Just look in the direction of David Bowie, resurgent, almost pre-empting the new romantic posturing that was to follow on his *Scary Monsters, Super Creeps* LP. Diana Ross made her best album for years, Van Morrison released *Common One*, Stevie Wonder joined in on the social commentary via *Hotter than July* as he campaigned hard to get the United States to recognise Martin Luther King's Birthday as a national holiday. The Rolling Stones went disco, Bob Dylan turned to God whilst Bob Marley posed the question *Could you be Loved?* upon his *Uprising album* and even Queen released an half decent tune. Unquestionably the year delivered unique and unrepeatable creative peaks, there was a cultural crossroads, a melting pot of ideas, experimental, enduring, exciting. The sixties flaunted but floundered, the seventies encouraged indulgence, punk paved the way but trust me...check the records, twelve golden months of music.1980 is where it's at.

Let's just take a moment to look at some of the music that got released in the year I became a teenager, I believe it's why I became an obsessive, an incurable. Check this out –

The Clash – *Sandinista*
The Jam – *Sound Affects*
Dexys Midnight Runners – *Searching For the Young Soul Rebels*
The Pretenders – *The Pretenders*
The Cure – *Boys Don't Cry*
Linton Kwesi Johnson – *Bass Culture*
Magazine – *The Correct Use of Soap*
Elvis Costello & the Attractions – *Get Happy*
The Beat – *I Just Can't Stop It*
The Selecter – *Too Much Pressure*
Squeeze – *Argybargy*
Stiff Little Fingers – *Nobody's Heroes*
Talking Heads – *Remain in Light*
XTC – *Black Sea*
Devo – *Freedom of Choice*
Grace Jones – *Warm Leatherette*
Siouxsie and the Banshees – *Kaleidoscope*
The Undertones – *Hypnotised*
Dead Kennedys – *Fresh Fruit for Rotting Vegetables*
The Teardrop Explodes – *Kilimanjaro*
Echo & the Bunnymen – *Crocodiles*

Joy Division – *Closer*
John Cooper Clarke – *Snap, Crackle & Bop*
UB40 – *Signing Off*
Adam and the Ants – *Kings of the Wild Frontier*
The Cure – *Seventeen Seconds*
The Human League – *Travelogue*
The Chords – *So Far Away*
The Cramps – *Songs the Lord Taught Us*
Secret Affair – *Behind Closed Doors*
The Ruts – *Grin and Bear It*
Suicide – *Suicide*
David Bowie – *Scary Monsters, Super Creeps*
Pere Ubu – *The Art of Walking*
The B-52's – *Wild Planet*
Zapp – *Zapp*
Black Uhuru – *Sinsemilla*
Kate Bush – *Never for Ever*
Madness – *Absolutely*
Kurtis Blow – *Kurtis Blow*
Skids – *The Absolute Game*
The Police – *Zenyatta Mondatta*
Prince – *Dirty Mind*
Thin Lizzy – *Chinatown*
AC/DC – *Back in Black*
The Monochrome Set – *Love Zombies*
U2 – *Boy*
The Damned – *The Black Album*
The Specials – *More Specials*
John Lennon and Yoko Ono – *Double Fantasy*
The Fall – *Grotesque*
Breaking Glass *Original Soundtrack*
Sham 69 – *The Game*
Stiff Little Fingers – *Hanx*
Burning Spear – *Live in Dub*

The Plasmatics – *Butcher Baby EP*
Zounds – *Can't Cheat Karma EP*
The Jam – *Going Underground* 7"
A Certain Ratio – *Shack up* 7"
The Human League – *Being Boiled* 7"
Gang of Four – *Yellow EP*

Joan Armatrading – *Me, Myself, I* 7"
Lipps Inc – *Funkytown* 7"
Diana Ross – *Upside Down* 7"
Blondie – *Rapture* 7"
Queen – *Another one Bites the Dust* 7"
David Bowie – *Ashes to Ashes* 7"
Jona Lewie – *You'll Always Find me in the Kitchen at Parties* 7"
The Jacksons – *Can You Feel It* 7"
The Lambrettas – *Poison Ivy* 7"
Gary Numan – *Cars* 7"
The Rolling Stones – *Emotional Rescue* 7"
The Stranglers – *Who wants the World* 7"
Talking Heads – *Once in a Lifetime* 7"
Motorhead – *Ace of Spades* 7"
The Clash – *Bankrobber* 7"
Martha and the Muffins – *Echo Beach* 7"
OMD – *Enola Gay* 7"
The Korgis – *Everybody's got to Learn Sometime* 7"
Dead Kennedys – *Holiday in Cambodia* 7"
George Benson – *Give me the Night* 7"
Josef K – *It's kind of Funny* 7"
Orange Juice – *Simply Thrilled Honey* 7"
Joy Division – *Love will Tear us Apart* 7"
The Stray Cats – *Runaway Boys* 7"
The Ruts – *Staring at the Rude Boys* 7"
The Vapours – *Turning Japanese* 7"
The Chords – *The British Way of Life* 7"
Secret Affair – *My World* 7"
The Specials – Live EP feat – *Too Much Too Young* 7"
The Specials – *Do Nothing* 7"
The Specials – *Stereotypes / International Jet Set* 7"

I have probably missed hundreds, it is not intended as a definitive list, just a few things that sit amongst my record collection but I am sure you get the picture.

4 – OUT ON THE FLOOR

Absolute Beginners, obsessives, incurables ... call it what you will, but both me and Hammy had been smitten and bitten by the bug. There would be no turning back, and ever-increasingly we would spend almost every waking hour, when we hadn't got the inconvenience of school, in each other's company. We sourced books, newspaper cuttings, films, and of course records, tracing it all backwards in order to move forwards. Paul Weller would name-drop The Five Stairsteps, Shuggie Otis or The Action in the *NME*. That weekend we'd catch the bus into one of the big towns or cities and attempt to unearth these treasures, or seek out Impressions records, *Stax Records*, 60s beat groups … and Dexys Midnight Runners, who we absolutely adored, with their distinctive, powerful sound and imagery, covered *Seven Days Is Too Long*, *Breaking Down The Walls Of Heartache* and *The Horse*. In turn, we became acquainted with Chuck Woods, Jimmy Johnson and Cliff Nobles & Co. But whereas most of our peers were happy enough to don a parka and a pair of sta-prest, or watch *Quadrophenia* over and over again, we wanted to discover more, to dig deeper, to go back to the source, the roots of this movement that had just come from leftfield and swept us off our feet. Soul music, it became our thing.

While conversing and plotting our next adventure to buy whatever threads or platters that held our attention at the time, we would meet and hang out in cafés, mainly to feed our teenage addiction for tea. Sometimes we'd fill our faces with a chip batch (that may be buttie/roll/cob/barm cake to you, depending on what region of the country you get your bread buttered) but eating seemed almost like an inconvenience to us, plus it was money that could be put towards another Smokey Robinson LP, or a pair of brogues. Even when the caffs were shut on Sunday, we would still have a drop-in centre to get our *Typhoo* fix. While having a walk out 'n' about, we'd use the local train station or the swimming baths. Now, it was while sipping away at Atherstone swimming baths one fateful afternoon that our eyes would be well and truly opened to the weird and wonderful world of northern soul. Hammy knew one of the pool attendants reasonably well, Paul "Mitch" Mitchell. Mitch was several years older than us but grew up on the same estate. He was on a break from his poolside duties this day, and sidled over to our table in the reception area, where we were sat with two plastic cups of our fortnightly (too weak) brew. After an initial bit of banter, teasing and ribbing us for our well-groomed appearance, he seemed impressed at how far we'd go to obtain knowledge of records, and these two young lads' attention to detail. Mitch then dropped it on us. How did we fancy going to a real soul do? An all-nighter? Non-Stop Dancing. A twilight world of rare soul music. stompers, floaters, baggies, talc, towels, holdalls, backdrops, acrobatics, amphetamines, hand-claps, *Keep The Faith* and a new religion. A Way of Life.

Where?

Hinckley.

Hinckley? Fucking Hinckley? I think we both spilt our brew. Hinckley was where my Auntie Pam lived, just down the A5. A sleepy two-horse market town like ours and Mitch is telling us that hundreds of like-minded folk travel the length and breadth of the country to attend. Furthermore, to add to our astonishment, he tells us they've just had Jr. Walker on, and the next one that's planned will feature none other than Curtis Mayfield! If we fancy it, give him a shout, and we may be able to get a lift over, he's sure we'll get in as long as we keep our heads down and cause no fuss.

We're buzzing! This is the real deal. A northern soul all-nighter, and on our doorstep! Then reality hits. This is 1982, Hammy's barely fifteen, I'm fourteen, we're still at school, and we're planning on fucking off to Hinckley with grown blokes we only loosely know, to a dance that doesn't begin until midnight, and doesn't finish until 8 a.m. on Sunday morning. This is going to take some planning. To our surprise, it was fairly straightforward. I would tell my parents that I'm staying at Hammy's for the night, and he'd tell his parents that he's staying over at mine. Simple. As long as neither parent phoned for any reason, we'd be fine. Before we knew it, we were in the back of a car travelling the short journey down the A5 to Hinckley. Mitch's mate and fellow poolside lifeguard Steve drove. I vividly recall being overcome with excitement and anticipation, but also intoxicated with nerves, made all the more apparent by the fact that driver Steve only had one arm and he was currently travelling at 100mph like James Hunt at the *Monaco Grand Prix!* This was probably more to do with the amphetamines that he'd just swallowed rather than any desire to become the first one-armed Formula 1 champion.

The venue was also an unlikely location. It was at the leisure centre, usually used for public swimming and sporting activities. We arrived slightly early, just before the doors were due to open, and already queues had formed. An odd-looking bunch gathered, an unlikely mix, although I'm not sure what I expected. Sharp threads were a secondary consideration. These types had their own codes. Oxford bags, Spencers, brogues, embroidered patches both on holdalls and jackets, club patches, sometimes attached to blazers, shirts and vests. The music and dancing was king here. As I approached the hall's entrance doors, I was certain that we, or at least I, would be refused entrance. We'd never really been served at a bar before, but that didn't matter here. No alcohol was on sale, purely soft drinks. Anyway, as I'd later come to find, most were too speeded out of their minds on uppers to get bogged down with ale. We just kept our heads down, carried on moving, paid our fiver in, and walked through the doors into the main hall.

As history now tells us, this was probably the third wave of the northern soul scene. The original golden era of *The Torch* and Manchester's *Twisted Wheel* was just a distant memory, and the legendary *Wigan Casino* had closed its doors for the last time in 1981. But we'd been far too young for any of that. Hell, we were still too young now really, but for us this was *Year Zero*, our introduction, our first entrance into that spellbinding kingdom of soul. That night, the dancefloor was heaving; this is where the magic happened. We gazed on in wonder at this packed, pulsating floor. Watching some of the dancers perform, (and that's what it's like, a performance, a show), was like observing a work of art. Again, codes, routines and a certain etiquette were involved. They would casually warm up, and even that looked effortlessly cool. Gliding, sliding, spinning, then as the music found its way through the gears, the drum-breaks, choruses and vocal shouts would be met with a series of acrobatic moves, backdrops, flips, drops, handclaps. I was mesmerised by it, and had seen nothing quite like it before. It took a few more visits until I participated fully, having practiced my moves, trying them out in the privacy of my bedroom. You had to respect that dancefloor, not just clumsily barge straight onto it. There was so much for us to take in on that first visit, from the dancing, to the attire, to the extraordinary music pumping across the hall, that Curtis Mayfield's performance that night was almost a sideshow. Right there and then, I'd immediately fallen in love with this secret, underground world of northern soul. It was obsessive, passionate, consuming, forever changing, totally in step with my young modernist attitudes. Daylight was soon seeping through, and Dean

Parrish's anthem *I'm On My Way* signaled the culmination of my first experience of an all-nighter. As we stepped out to the harsh, bright morning sunlight, I felt delirious with excitement, informed and enlightened by the eight hours that I'd just witnessed. I couldn't wait to return, to learn more, and to belong.

Over the next few years, I hardly missed an event that promoter Chris King put on in Hinckley, and we even spread our wings and ventured further afield to venues in Stafford and Stoke. By now our parents had rumbled us. We'd come clean about our all-night escapades, and they had begrudgingly given us the nod to continue our adventures, knowing we would more than likely find a way out anyway. I made many good friends during this period, all regular attendees of all-nighters and soul devotees who I'm still close to. I was lucky enough to see many legendary artists perform; the leisure centre was a real draw for putting live acts on, artists such as Major Lance, Martha Reeves, Edwin Starr and the wonderful Ric-Tic Revue, which also included JJ Barnes, Al Kent, Pat Lewis and Lou Ragland. That particular night, I remember the venue being absolutely rammed. On one occasion I recall queuing in the freezing cold, nervously waiting to gain entry to the leisure centre when Eddie Holman was due to perform. I say nervously, because I was still fairly young at this point, and didn't want to draw any unnecessary attention to myself. But word had got out amongst some of our Atherstone associates, and a couple of others had tagged along on this occasion. One I knew I could trust not to play up, but the other, Tommy, was a wildcard, and was already fairly inebriated with alcohol. Not cool. As we passed the doorman, my intoxicated friend enquired in somewhat slurred tones "Ay up mate, busy tonight, innit? Who's on?"
"The Holman." came the reply.

Tommy sounded horrified. "Fuckin' hell, not fucking Marc Almond?" I cringed and hastily made my way in, trying to shake off any association with Tommy. Despite his naïve ignorance and drunken swagger he was allowed entry, and proceeded to fall asleep in the nearest corner until turning out time. As time passed, the scene started to change again. Hinckley also switched venue to the nearby *Regent Club*; I think the growth of sporting commitments at the leisure centre made it difficult to book regular nights, and the all-nighters became more sporadic. Some odd, more current names at the time popped up to guest as DJs at the *Regent Club*. People like Stephen "Tin Tin" Duffy, and JoBoxer/Subway Sect drummer Sean McLusky. Around 1985, there was a shift towards the tasteless psychobilly scene, spearheaded by bands like King Kurt and The Meteors. Some of these undesirables filtered into the northern soul scene, more via scooter rallies than all-nighters at first, but soon enough there were divides, and the scene cooled off a little for a while.

There has always been an extraordinary bond between the music of Black America and the lifestyle of the working class British incurable; it's part of that traditional searing modernist aesthetic. In more recent times, due to my involvement with playing and writing music with Stone Foundation, I have been fortunate enough to work and record with several renowned and respected American soul artists, including Steve Calloway of 60s Detroit vocal harmony group The Professionals, and the wonderful Nolan Porter. Also Joe Harris, front man of both the Fabulous Peps (who regularly opened for James Brown at his famous *Harlem Apollo* shows) and Motown legends The Undisputed Truth. It was kind of weird for me travelling full circle over a thirty-year period, discovering and becoming fascinated with all aspects of soul music, then finally getting to work and develop friendships with these great characters. Some nights, both in rehearsals and on stage, the band would be playing together with these unique and genuine voices of soul, and we'd have to just glance over at each other to see that we were all thinking the same thing, all of us caught in that 'pinch yourself' moment. In 2011 we did a live radio session for the *Craig Charles Soul and Funk Show* for *BBC 6 Music* with Joe, and I got so lost in the music and listening to Joe Harris literally pour his heart and soul into that recording, that I almost forget that it was a live broadcast and I was playing bass on the session, the fan in me was totally engaged in just listening to Joe sing.

On these visits to the UK they were enthralled by the knowledge, passion, devotion and appreciation that they encountered from the underground soul fraternity. They were more excited, inspired, spirited and jubilant to be singing now than they have ever been, once again an example of Black American soul and r 'n' b music being reinvented, rediscovered, forever changing. This spirit will always live on.

5 - LONG HOT SUMMER - I PREDICT A RIOT

1983 was simply a magical year! Sometimes, if I open up the windows, I can smell it drifting back to engage my senses once more. Its spirit has never really left me. For this was the year of the *Long Hot Summer*. This was the year that gave birth to The Style Council. On reflection, I find it remarkable that in less than twelve months, Paul Weller went from waxing lyrical with disgruntled observations about a *Town Called Malice*, to soundtracking the endless summer of 1983. From the off, I dug the Style Council. Right age, right time perhaps? Also, it was exciting to be right there at the start of something new. Of course, the news of Paul Weller's decision to call time on The Jam had shocked and saddened a nation of young kids with modernist tendencies. My heart sank, and I even shed a tear in *Gale's Newsagents* as I read the statement and news of their imminent split. They had given me the strength, belief and confidence to feel like I was somebody, at such a young age. Great groups will define their time and place in musical history, and The Jam defined ours. The Jam continued that long tradition of dynamic British pop groups – The Beatles, The Stones, The Kinks, The Who, Small Faces etc. ... The Jam belong in that great classification; it's the very reason we're still talking about them today, and with no shoddy reunions or comebacks to tarnish their legacy, that memory will hopefully always remain intact.

I honestly cannot think of one other band from that era you could say that about. Even The Clash made one album too many. I could put on a Jam record today and I am almost instantly reminded of that golden period. Huddled around a portable radio on a school lunch time, listening to the new single *Funeral Pyre*, rushing to buy the *NME* to find they had cleaned up in every category in the readers polls. Taping the charts on a Sunday to find out if they had gone in at No.1 and being cautioned at school for wearing a mohair suit ("It's not strictly school uniform is it, Sheasby lad?"). Pissing my 'O' level English literature exam, as it asked us to write a short piece by choosing one of the following titles, one of which was *Down In The Tube Station At Midnight*. As anyone who has ever witnessed them live would confirm, a Jam gig was not just another show. In fact, it was not a show at all, it was the real deal, it was an event. The sound that the three of them made was immensely powerful, which also must stand as a testament to the often-overlooked abilities and aptitudes of Foxton and Buckler. They were an absolute powerhouse, and the force and directness of those songs played live at a thunderous volume was just immense; a colossal sound, created by just three people. The atmosphere it generated was just magical. I don't think I've ever felt anything like it since. I wasn't one to mourn their passing for too long though, and in hindsight, Weller's judgement has proved to be spot on, plus he had new musical avenues to explore, which he (rightly) felt he couldn't pursue or achieve within the confines of The Jam.

I loved those early days of The Style Council. I can kind of understand why it rubbed some of the hardcore Jam Army fan-base up the wrong way, as it did seem like a reaction to all that had passed before, and the Council weren't really a group at all so to speak. In their formative days they comprised a nucleus of Weller and one-time Dexys Midnight Runner Mick Talbot (OK, I know he was only part of the early Runners for a fleeting moment, but it did seem like a good omen to me at the time, and I conveniently wanted to dismiss the fact that he'd been in The Merton Parkas). They would team up with whoever they so desired, to fit whatever song or vibe they were creating. It was a refreshing and unique approach. The early images of them, portrayed as ambassadors of some hip cappuccino-sipping young European stylists immersed in jazz and soul sounds, was ultra-cool and ultra-mod. It was all very anti-rock, which I loved. They spoke volumes to Hammy and I. Our ship came in. It was a *headstart for happiness*.

1983, and the birth of The Style Council seemed to open up our senses. Although it was a heavily-politicised period, in the wake of Thatcher's ever-increasing 'divide and rule' vice-like grip on the country, it was an optimistic time, and our minds were tuned to the vision of a thousand possibilities. Thirty years later, truth be told, I don't feel all that different. There's always a new song to be heard, or a new style to explore, but back then my head was buoyed with expectation. It was as if a whole bunker of culture, both past and present, was opening in front of us. It was a year of excitement and discovery. The Style Council were as fresh as the scent of a newly mown summer lawn, as cool as a mountain stream. The first photo shoot was in Boulogne, northern France, young Europeans, ultra-Mod coolness personified. I recall the *Speak like a Child* video being shot in the Malvern Hills, and thinking wow! That's only sixty miles away from me! If only I'd known that Paul Weller was making a video with his new band just sixty miles up the road! (I'm not sure what I thought was going to happen, but at fifteen your imagination knows no bounds). Nick Barker teased me on the school playground. He had heard an exclusive play on late-night *Radio 1* of *Money-Go-Round*. ("It's fucked up funk Sheas, he's kind of rapping! You're gonna love it!" - I did, and I still do). This was the year of what seemed like a never-ending *Long Hot Summer*, and that very record, the *Á-Paris EP*, soundtracked the days, with Hammy and I in his tiny council estate bedroom, dreaming of starting our own musical adventures, windows open wide, the aroma of summer filtering in. *The Paris Match* and *Party Chambers*; we would play that EP over and over, spend hours staring at that sleeve. Stunning modernist imagery, Weller dressed to perfection. 1983 was also the last time I went on holiday with just my mum and dad. We went to Bournemouth, and still the heat poured down from above. It was here in the hotel TV room that I watched The Style Council perform on *Top Of the Pops* (*The Paris Match*) and went out (alone) that very night to hear Steve Wright DJ on the Pier. I danced (alone) to the full 12-inch version of *Long Hot Summer*, currently nestling at No. 3 in the hit parade.

The school holiday lasted forever, the days seemed endless and time stood still. Myself and Hammy were still enjoying our own courtship days, hardly spending a single day apart from each other, always swapping ideas and opinions. We'd spend afternoons chasing girls, two in particular – Sonia and Cheryl - we didn't always have enough spare change to catch the Baddesley Bomber up the hill, so we'd walk the 5 mile or so round trip. Sonia and Cheryl were best friends, which made it even more convenient and attractive to us that we could pair up, and wouldn't have to spend too much time away from each other (me and Hammy that is, not our respective girlfriends). They too were into music, which was something of a deal clincher; not the Council though, they had their own thing going on. I remember them being heavily into Heaven 17 and the Tears for Fears first album *The Hurting*. We also heard ABC and Haircut 100 on more than a few of our sojourns up to Baddesley, which if I'm honest we didn't mind too much. The other big tunes that soundtracked that summer were *Love Town* by Booker Newberry III and *I.O.U* by Freeez; we really dug those two grooves. Most girls of our age around this time were decked out ridiculously, sporting rah-rah skirts and pixie boots, but thankfully, Sonia and Cheryl didn't succumb to such fashion atrocities. They were kind of cool in their own way, and we dated for quite some time. I think Hammy's relationship with Cheryl endured a lot longer than mine and Sonia's.

I was far too busy basking in the glory of becoming a part-time pop star to get tied down in any long-term teenage romance. We had even made the dizzy heights of the *Tamworth Herald's Musicbox* column, and our band was the talk of the playground for at least a week. Some bright spark, one of our mates, but I unfortunately can't recall who, had ventured out one evening armed with a can of spray-paint and redecorated the bench outside the swimming baths with our band's name 'The In-Crowd', but by the time *the Herald* sent their photographer to capture us, all modded-up, looking mean and moody, we had shortened our group's title to 'The Crowd', so we had to position Hammy strategically just so he would cover up the word "In" on the photograph.

It could have been easy to be ridiculed for attempting to take our band's efforts seriously but most people, both the kids at school and some of the teachers, were quite supportive, which was not only a surprise, but also a vote of confidence. One particular teacher was very encouraging of our musical endeavours, and in fact, he was a complete breath of fresh air, compared to the general stuffy old teaching methods. He was a German called Torsten Friedag, and he became my form teacher. From the first moment he walked through the classroom door, he said "Please don't call me Sir, or Mr. Friedag, my name is Torsten". He owned a scooter too, so we hit it off straight away. I attended secondary school just at the fag-end of having to tolerate the old guard, the ones that thought it was OK to rap your knuckles with a steel ruler, throw chalk at your head or even cane you. We had a few cunts like that, and Torsten must have been quite a shock to their system. His teaching methods were fairly inspired, and he certainly had wise ways for one so young (I would put him at around thirty when he started at our school). You would want to work for him, there weren't many who played him up, he respected the kids, and in turn he got respect back.

I remember he once installed a record player in the classroom, and told everyone to think of a song that meant something to them and to bring it in the next day; the words would have to relate in some way to your life. I suppose this was something of a challenge for a room full of fourteen-year-olds. It must have been, because only about five of us returned the next day clutching records. I didn't need much encouraging, and jumped at the chance to pose all day with an album under my arm. I took in *The Who By Numbers* LP and played *How Many Friends Have I Really Got?* It struck a chord with Torsten, as I think it was just the kind of thought-provoking response he was looking for. We hit it off ever since that moment, and once he found out that I was in a band, he not only encouraged it, but also arranged for us to rehearse in the school hall, which we did every Tuesday evening and Sunday afternoon. The on-site caretaker would open up for us, and that arrangement, thanks to Torsten, lasted for many years, way after I had left school too. Torsten also arranged for us to stage a concert and play a gig for the students at the annual school disco. There was a video of it once upon a time, but I think I lent it out and it never got returned; shame, as it was a cracker of a gig. Oddly enough, I ended up living in Torsten's old house on Coleshill Road for a while. He even threw a couple of parties for us here, which would be strictly taboo in these politically correct times. I still have a James Brown album of his that I shamefully never returned.

He turned up on TV a few years back, as some kind of superhead teacher, where he was attempting to solve widespread problems in North London schools, and it was via this programme that I was able to actually gain contact with him once again. I sent him an e-mail and reminded him of how gracious and helpful he had been, and that I was still mining that musical seam almost thirty years later. I could fully appreciate now how important his influence on me had been, and I wanted to tell him so. He was equally delighted to hear from me, and was happy to know that my family had settled in his old abode in Atherstone. He was flattered by my words, and asked if we could possibly hook up once again, now that we were both grown men, and I no longer his pupil. We arranged to meet, he was scheduled to come and visit us, but then almost immediately the e-mails stopped. Three weeks later, I read in the pages of the *Tamworth Herald* (ironically) that a former teacher at *Atherstone High School* had died suddenly from a stroke. It was Torsten. As saddening and sobering as this news was, I was pleased that I'd had the opportunity to express my gratitude for his guidance. He broke down barriers, and set an example that I will never forget.

Our youthful musical potential also didn't go unnoticed amongst other local bands. Most of them suffered the professional jealousy syndrome, especially the old rock farts, who considered themselves part of some sort of hierarchy. They weren't too keen on a gang of young upstarts stealing their thunder and their column inches in the local rags. We did however find some kindred spirits within our neighbouring scene in the form of psychedelic modernists The Dream Factory, who at the time were being courted by several record companies, and were rapidly becoming popular amongst the developing scooterist fraternity. The Dream Factory were led by a fellow-bass player by the name of Mark Mortimer, and it was he who gave us our first handful of credible gigs, supporting his band, consequently becoming another key figure in encouraging and championing us in those formative days. He seemed to warm to me and Hammy straight away; I guess we had similar tastes. It was around this time that Hammy and I were delving deeper into all the various offshoots and elaborations of the mod vibe, which led us to embrace psychedelia. Our discovery of *The Crazy World Of Arthur Brown* LP had blown our minds, and in turn, that created a pathway to Pink Floyd's *Piper At The Gates Of Dawn*, and then on to the US psych and garage groups like The Seeds, Love, 13th Floor Elevators, The Chocolate Watch Band and The Electric Prunes. Mortimer was suitably impressed with the dedication of his young protégées; we had common ground and a mutual respect, which I hasten to add is something that remains between me and Mark to this day (he has recently enjoyed success with his band DC Fontana).

I suppose you have fathomed by now that staying loyal to the strict codes and guidelines of a young mod's regime was proving difficult for me. It could be a confusing affair, I was still a pup of course, and learning all the time, but I had become intoxicated with music. I loved the many different aspects of it, and could easily embrace the lure of many genres. Already you may have noticed that I could be as equally enthralled by electro-poppers Freeez as I could by the 'God Of Hell Fire' Arthur Brown. I didn't get too hung up on it though. Paul Weller helped us out somewhat by voicing his appreciation of Spandau Ballet's *Chant No.1* and Culture Club's *Colour By Numbers* LP, so I figured if 'the guv'nor' is allowed to travel off the beaten track, then it must be OK for me to dig Aztec Camera (who were undeniably great anyway), and play *Our Lips Are Sealed* by the Fun Boy Three on repeat. Surely, the very essence of modernism is to keep one eye on the past while constantly moving forward and evolving? The confines of nostalgia have constantly blighted the scene over the years. These days, some gatherings I have played at have resembled an Austin Powers fancy dress party.

One lamentable incident sticks in my mind more than any, while I was attempting to work out what was and was not acceptable for a fourteen-year-old mod kid to consider cool. A lad called Shaun Major came bounding over to me all enthusiastically one break time, top playground. I remember it as if it were yesterday, as I'm still kicking myself about it three decades on. "Hey Sheas, you love your music don't ya' mate? Do you fancy going to see Thin Lizzy at *Brum Odeon* tonight? We've got a spare ticket, it's yours if you want it". Of course, the obvious answer was 'yes' and 'great, thanks for thinking of me' ... What came out of my mouth?

"Why the fuck would I want to go and see that shit? Stood amongst a bunch of bastard grebos, watching a fucking rocker's band?!" Poor old Shaun, who really is the most affable, likeable and unpretentious soul you could ever have the good fortune to meet, looked at me in astonishment and disappointment. "Major, I'm a mod mate, I can't be seen dead at a gig like that". Of course, I thought Thin Lizzy were a great rock 'n' roll band, probably the pick of the bunch; they had soul, and great songs. Shortly after that rebuffed invite Phil Lynott was dead, and Lizzy were over. Not one of my better decisions. The things we do for mod, eh?

After our band's little feature in the local paper, interest in our teenage beat combo had started to gather pace. We had put an ad out to expand our line-up and augment it with a brass section and a keyboard player. Somewhat surprisingly, we were flooded with expressions of interest. Well, we had at least five, one of which was from a female Hammond organ player. She was a girl in our school year, one most of us had a crush on too, a good-looking girl who covered her Maths book with pictures of The Jam, so that just made her even more attractive to me, and I didn't even know she could play the organ by this point. Amanda Smith had only one rehearsal with us. It was obvious from the off that it wasn't going to work out. Musically, she was actually fine, quite competent and grasped the songs with ease. It actually sounded great. The problem we had was apparent immediately, as we placed her right at the front of the stage, and all stood in a line directly behind her to maximize our vantage point, all the better to witness her backside bobbing up and down as she fingered the mighty organ (sorry, I couldn't help that one) – Seriously it was a like a scene from a *Carry On* film, or *On The Buses*. It was just plain wrong. We'd have fallen out over her after two weeks of that. We decided to stick to running our band as a boys' club only. I don't think she was too gutted, or lost any sleep about not passing her audition.

The summer before I left school, which was the May of '84, The Crowd were invited by Mark Mortimer to support them at their gig at the Arts Centre in Tamworth. It was a kind of a last hurrah for us all before leaving school. Loads of our mates turned up for the event, and the tiny theatre was rammed way over its capacity. Everyone stood, the seats were just discarded, which made for a real sense of occasion, and it was one that we more than rose to. It was probably the definitive moment in us all deciding to pursue the band thing. Don't get me wrong, I was dedicated and hooked on it already, but so many young bands get no further than six months of rehearsals in their parents' garage, a couple of gigs to show off to their mates, then jack it all in and spend the next forty years of their lives boasting that they were in a band once. It's been a way of life to me, an integral part of who I am, but if no-one had been bothered or interested on that summer's night at *Tamworth Arts Centre* then maybe, just maybe, it would have been a very different story. But as it was, people were interested, very much so, and we tore the fucking roof off the place. Tamworth Herald's *Musicbox* supremo Sam Holliday had this to say in the following weeks newspaper – "They are young, energetic and full of genuine feeling and passion for their music. Their relative youth only served to make their tight, well-co-ordinated sound even more impressive, with a great smattering of original soulful songs. It's clear that they are a band with a great future. In fact they are a perfect example of the type of band Paul Weller is now championing – *Dig The New Breed* indeed!" Not exactly Charles Shaar Murray racking off in the *NME* about us, I know, but to us it meant everything. It added combustion to our compulsion. Sam wasn't just blowing smoke up our young arses either. Once again the night was filmed (by Torsten actually), and I do still have an old battered *VHS* copy of it on video as a keepsake, and I can honestly say the older I get the more incredible that footage seems. Phil can barely see over the top of his drum kit, he's only thirteen, or something ridiculous! Hammy looks super-cool, fronting it like he's a veteran, both of us resplendent in our mohair suits. I am really quite proud of it.

Not every gig ended in such triumph though. Only a few months later in, October of the same year, the band was approached to play in our hometown, a big concert that would be staged at *Atherstone Memorial Hall*. It was to have a late licence, a kind of post-pub gig. After kicking-out time was always a risky affair, especially on a Friday night, in what was then a bustling town-centre full of drinkers who would use any excuse to get a late beer or two somewhere, regardless of what was happening. I think it was the local rugby club that organised it, so really we should have known better, but £100 was the agreed fee, and to be fair, none of us had even seen a hundred pounds before; it sounded like a King's ransom. What could possibly go wrong? We had just recently decided to change the name of our band from the rather dull and unadventurous moniker of "The Crowd" to the more fitting, colourful but nevertheless ridiculous title of "Dance Stance". Mine and Hammy's Dexys obsession still held a firm grip, and we hit upon what we considered the genius idea of re-naming ourselves after Dexys Midnight Runners' first single. I mean, who would remember that? It was almost four years since its release, and even the band had changed the song's title to *Burn It Down* for its inclusion on the album. I can't even remember if we informed the rest of the band, to be honest. It probably just appeared on the posters, flanked by a tiny footnote, with "Formerly known as The Crowd" in brackets.

What we didn't really account for was the fact that we would no longer be playing in front of our teenage mates in the comfort of a local Arts Centre theatre. This was a post-midnight piss-up, full of grown-up geezers and women, mostly pissed out of their minds already, and intent on making the most of a late bar after the rest of the boozers in town had turfed everyone out. What they probably didn't expect was to be entertained by an hour's set from an underage mod band, complete with trumpets, trombones and Hammond organ. It was a weird vibe right from the off, and I honestly don't think it made the slightest jot of difference whether we were playing or not. You put four hundred tanked-up punters in a room full of tits and testosterone, and something is bound to give. It wasn't exactly on par with Altamont, but what ensued has gone down in local folklore as *The Memorial Hall Riot*. At least that's how the front pages of all the local papers described it in the aftermath. In reality, it was just a punch-up between three or four blokes that escalated into a free-for-all. Our set lasted no more than fifteen minutes, and we were about three songs into the set when it all kicked off. To make matters worse, a few knobheads were trying to grab the microphone stands to use as weapons to wrap around somebody's head. Nick (Thomas) took full advantage of his elevated position on the high stage and booted one of them straight full on in the face. Glasses got thrown, and before too long just about everybody in the hall was rucking. It was some sight to behold. I think I was quoted in the paper as saying I was "upset, sickened and disgusted" by the events and the behaviour. Truth be told, it didn't do our reputation or esteem in the area too much harm at all. Once again, we were the name on everyone's lips on the local scene. We thought it best to lie low for a few weeks. As I said previously, we didn't really get caught up in attempting to get served in pubs before our time like a lot of youths our age did. We'd rather stay in and play sounds all night, but on one of mine, Hammy and Nick's rare ventures uptown (top ranking) for a few swift illicit shandies, we were greeted like returning heroes of war. The headline news of the "riot" stories had propelled us to regional infamy.

It wasn't just the macho dialogue of men that we attracted either; somehow, that night ended with me propped up against the bar of *the Clock* (*White Lion*, remember) getting along famously with a girl almost twice my age (well, that's a bit of an exaggeration, but she was in her early twenties). I think I got quite confident, and after a couple of light ales, I suddenly remembered that we were staying at Nick's house, as his mum and dad were away on holiday. 'Perfect', I thought. I invited her round. Nick cracked open the drinks cabinet, and then somewhat bizarrely decided to put on a *Betamax* copy of the film *Caligula*, which is famed for being the first major motion picture to feature semi pornographic scenes. So, there's me, Hammy, Nick and this girl we don't really know at all, getting wrecked on Lorna and Jim's *Southern Comfort*, watching a movie about a Roman orgy. It could have been awkward, but she seems happily engrossed in ogling the scenes from the bordello on the box.

"I bet you couldn't do that", I offer.

"What?" she retorts.

"Do as the Roman's do."

"I bet I could."

Hammys got his head in his hands in disbelief, and Nick's just about jogging on the spot with excitement. "Go on then", I continue, laying down the bait.

"Sheas!" Nick interrupts "I'm all out of booze! We've caned my mum and dad's *Southern Comfort*."

"Why don't we go down to my house?", offers our accommodating twenty-something. "There's no-one in" she teases, "and I've got plenty to drink."

Within minutes, we find ourselves trekking off to a stranger's house in search of alcohol and *Caligula*-esque sex. Nick's virtually running down the road, and insists upon repeatedly shaking my hand and asking me if I mind, as if this girl who appears to be game-on for tackling the *Three Musketeers* is my fucking new girlfriend or something. What the hell do I care? Let's get pissed and see what happens. Hammy meanwhile, is dragging his heels, shaking his head at me in astonishment. "What the fuck are we doing here?" he says, to no-one in particular, as we find ourselves in the girl's kitchen, drinking anything we can get our hands on.

"I'll just go upstairs get myself comfortable. Come up in ten minutes boys ..."

I feel like I'm in a movie now (*The Graduate*) as our host makes her way up to the bedroom. Nick's celebrating like he's won a *World Cup*-winners' medal, and we're all inebriated by this point, but nothing's gonna stop us climbing those stairs to find out what's in store. We kind of fall up the steps, all trying to suppress our childish giggling, we open the bedroom door, and fair play to her, there she is, lying on the bed, sporting only next week's washing. But then she makes one vital faux pas. She decides to put on some music to heighten the moment and sexually seduce us further; she rolls to one side of the bed and presses play on the portable cassette player. What seductive tunes did she have in store to arouse us? Marvin Gaye? Al Green?

Now, I'm not sure if she had checked what tape was jammed inside that cassette machine prior to us entering her boudoir, but it seems highly unlikely to me that an intimate foursome romp would be soundtracked by what was about to come blaring out of those speakers … Kid Creole and the Coconuts – "Welcome to the lifeboat party child, invitation only for the rank and file!" I couldn't see for the next ten minutes for the tears of laughter streaming down my face! I think our moment of shared intimacy had certainly passed, especially by the time we got to *Annie I'm Not Your Daddy!*

6 – SO, WHAT DO YOU WANT TO DO WHEN YOU LEAVE SCHOOL?

"So, what do you want to do when you leave school?"

I would hear those eleven words over and over. From teachers, my mum, my dad, aunties, uncles, aunties that I called Auntie but weren't really my auntie, they were just neighbours that had lived down our street since the beginning of time, even some of my mates, who were more than likely as clueless as me as to what the answer to that question should be. I just didn't have a clue. What was I supposed to say? All I wanted to do was play in a band, but they didn't have a *YTS* scheme for that career path. Time had just crept up on me. I hadn't even really considered leaving school, let alone life after it. I decided the best solution was to just shy away from that decision for a while, and enrol on a course at the local college, to give myself some time to think about it all. In a fashion not dissimilar to a game of 'pin the tail on the donkey', I randomly chose a two-year *BTEC* Diploma course in Business Studies as my excuse to fanny about all week. And fanny about I did too. Shame they didn't hand out degrees and diplomas in that.

The summer leading up to starting college heralded some changes, especially for the band. Nick Thomas never made it past the *Memorial Hall* incident; maybe some of the spirit was broken that night. A couple of the lads that played in the brass section left to begin life at university, but Hammy, Phil and I had tasted the euphoria of playing gigs, and also I think that the creative appeal of writing songs and bouncing ideas off each other appealed to us. We had only just begun. We weren't ready to throw the towel in now. So, we asked about, and went in search of kindred spirits.

Youth culture was embracing some radical changes too. For quite some time now, sports gear was creeping into vogue, beginning first on the football terraces. The casual subculture started in the late 1970s, after Liverpool fans introduced the rest of England to European fashions that they acquired while following their team during their *European Cup* campaigns of '77, '78 and '81. These fans returned to England with expensive Italian and French designer sportswear, most of which they had looted from stores. They brought back many new, unfamiliar (in the UK) clothing brands that had only been sported before by the likes of rising tennis stars such as Bjorn Borg and John McEnroe. Soon, other fans were clamouring for these rare items, such as *Fila* tops, *Lacoste* and *Sergio Tacchini* shirts, and unusual *Adidas* trainers. At the time, most police forces were still looking out for skinhead fans wearing *Dr. Marten* boots, and paid little attention to fans in expensive designer clothing. This new vogue quickly caught on, in London especially, and I witnessed first-hand evidence of it rapidly spreading through the kop at Elland Road in Leeds. If you were the sort of person who liked to keep one eye on your threads, you couldn't deny its influence on the streets of working-class towns and cities. Rival football gangs would not only want to outdo each other with their hooligan reputations, they now took pride in their wardrobe too. It wasn't long before it spilled over into the music scene, and the first unlikely pair to flirt with the casual dress code were Andrew Ridgley from Wham! and Aztec Camera's Roddy Frame, who was quick to sport a "wedge" haircut, but very soon swapped his *Fila* top for a tassel-fringed jacket.

I also took my first holiday abroad around this time, to Mallorca. Despite the rise of casual fashion, I was more caught up with the freshness and reconstruction of the modernist look that The Style Council had adopted, the young soul-stylist approach. I thought it was a great look, and I still do. This image also flirted with more feminine, pastel colours for men, even right down to your socks (if you wore any at all, of course), so on this first sojourn to Spain I returned with, amongst other items, two *Lacoste* cardigans, one lemon and the other a light pastel shade of pink, a new range for that season, and way off from hitting the shops back in the UK. I returned home quite pleased with my additions, and wore them proudly. That was until I donned the pink cardi to a Style Council *CND* gig at Coventry Apollo. It had been a great night (General Public had supported), and it was a real celebratory affair. Our friend Brownie had driven us over, and post-gig we walked out into the summer air, back to the car, jubilant, with a spring in our step, having just witnessed one of the best Council gigs of that period. No sooner had we got out of *the Apollo's* front doors and 100 yards down the main road than a gang of football casuals, walking in the opposite direction towards us, approached me. Without exaggeration, there would have been about fifteen of them, all aged between twenty and thirty. I was sixteen.

“Have you got the time, mate?” one of the ringleaders asked.
I knew instantly what was coming. “Nah mate sorry”. I tried to walk on.

“You a Fuckin’ Brummie?”

I didn’t even get the chance to respond before the punches started raining down on my head, fifteen of the fuckers onto a sixteen-year-old kid. I didn’t stand a chance. My first reaction was to curl up, to protect my face and teeth as much as I could, and take the beating. It soon became apparent that they were after the cardigan. ‘Taxing’, it was called. Why didn’t they just ask? It was probably covered in blood by the time they made off with it anyway. I was a mess. My face had still taken a severe battering despite my valiant efforts to shield it. I tracked back to *the Apollo* to seek help, and people just looked on aghast. I understand that it would have been futile for anyone to jump in and try and prevent it, and not for a moment did I think my mates had let me down. I, and anyone else for that matter, was on a hiding to nothing. They hunted in a pack, like fucking cowards. Safety in numbers. Picking on easy prey. As soon as the door staff at *the Apollo* saw me, they let me inside and no sooner had they done so, than the casual crew turned up again baying for more blood. Fuck knows what they wanted this time; probably my matching socks? Thankfully, an authoritative voice raced into the entrance of the venue and got staff to lock the doors. The police quickly arrived on the scene, forcing my assailants to scarper. I was in such a state that I hardly recognised the robust frame that had ordered the doors to be shut, who was now stood in front of me asking if I was OK, was anything broken?

“Let’s get you cleaned up, son.”

It was John Weller, Paul’s dad and manager. What a time to meet, eh? I took some solace in this, and the fact that my bones and teeth all seemed to be intact. I didn’t know what hurt most, the cuts and bruises, or being called a Brummie?

Fate conspired against those *Lacoste* cardigans. The other one, the light yellow one, was never quite the same after I decided to wear it on a visit to *Keresley Pit*. Hammy’s dad had received the invite, and the offer was extended to a couple more, whoever he chose to take along. So, he decided to take me and Hammy. I hadn’t really thought it through to be honest. An invitation to visit *Kerseley Colliery?* I just thought we were going to have a nose around the grounds, shake a few hands and get a lecture on the workings of a modern-day pit. I hadn't imagined that we would actually be going down the pit, to the coal face, a mile or so underground. I went dressed for the royal visit, handshakes and smiles, kitted out in my *Lacoste* buttoned knitwear. I turned up looking resplendent in lemon. Hammy and his dad just looked at me, jaws wide open. "Fucking hell, Sheas! ... we're going down the pit!" Ah well, I'm probably the best-dressed person in the history of coal mining ever to jump off a man-riding carriage.

The Delaney Brothers were semi casuals. I couldn't class them as full-on casuals, as they didn't embrace the violence at all, or even go to football matches that regularly, but they adopted the look. Dave was big on *Lacoste* and was an early convert to the wedge cut, while his younger brother Dick had a more laid-back style, *Kickers* and *Pringle* knitwear, which still leant towards that influence. I think they both arrived at the look via music, rather than the terraces of football stadiums. They dug Haircut 100, ABC, Animal Nightlife and other emerging Brit-funk bands like I-Level and Level 42 (anyone with 'Level' in their title ...)

Dave was a couple of years older than us, and a better musician than we had ever encountered up to this point. He had a groove and a swing to his guitar playing, although it must be said that the fact he had a beautiful red *Rickenbacker 360* guitar probably was the deal-clincher for us in deciding that he was our man. Dick was a bass-player, but our band didn't have a vacancy for that role, especially as I was handing out the positions, so Dick would play keyboards. I would go as far to say that the Delaney brothers were fairly accomplished by our standards, they could teach us a lot, and we were quick learners. With a nucleus of a five-piece band, Dance Stance were back in business, and ready to get moving once again after the false start of the "Riot" gig the previous year. Phil, Hammy and I were still determined to add a brass section to complete our sound. We were constantly hearing new music and groups that influenced our thinking, bands such as Working Week, Everything but the Girl, The Kane Gang, Big Sound Authority and The Redskins. By this time, we were always out at a gig too, catching all of the aforementioned plus many, many more. It was an inspiring time.

Initial rehearsals with our new musical comrades went well, really well. Our newfound buoyancy helped us decide it would be a good idea to make our first venture into the recording studio, and demo a couple of our new songs. Of course, we had to settle on the most expensive and professional studio we could find, which was *Horizon Studios* in Coventry. The Specials and The Selecter recorded here, and many of the legendary *2-Tone* recordings had been made here too. If we were looking to tap into the essence of those times, then we were in for a bit of a surprise. Video was in the midst of killing the radio star, and digital technology was selling everyone down the river; this was never more evident than in recording studios. We hoped to capture our sound, how we had been rehearsing for the past month or so, but no, our sound engineer and now self-proclaimed producer had other ideas for his guinea pigs. He had new toys to play with. For a start, the drum kit was disassembled, and stacked gathering dust in the corner of the live room. It had been replaced by black plastic pads shaped like fifty pence pieces. We must have spent a whole day getting the "sound" right on that crock of shit. I did point out that there was a real drum kit sat over in the corner, and couldn't we just set that up and record it instead of spending nine hours fine-tuning digital pads to sound like an actual drum kit? Mr Producer looked at me as if I was crazy. *Cupid And Psyche* by Scritti Politti had just been released and he played it relentlessly, heralding it as a genius work of modern production, which I didn't deny or argue with, but I hadn't really planned on taking Dance Stance down the synth-pop route anytime just yet.

Our would-be Trevor Horn at the controls was an unpleasant character too. He never ever wore any socks for the whole of the time we were in that studio, and he had toenails as long as your arm, like little blades sticking out from his feet. It was fucking repulsive. He also had the worst case of eczema I have ever encountered, and it even smelled. We really got short-changed, compromised and generally fucked about on that session. He ended up cajoling us into putting slap bass on one track. I was made to feel inferior because I simply couldn't play that way, and more to the point I didn't want to play that way. So Mr. Producer took me off the job and got Phil to play it instead. Slap bass, my arse. I should have slapped that sword-toed filthy motherfucker! We ended up with a cassette that sounded absolutely nothing like our band. It was more akin to a Howard Jones tribute act than the new soul vision we had been striving for. I was so disillusioned with my first experience of a proper recording studio. Surely, this wasn't what it was supposed to be like? As young and naïve as we were, I was determined never to put up with such bullshit again.

Hammy was now living above a pub, his mum and dad having taken over as landlords of *The Cricketers Arms* in Atherstone's Market Square. This certainly had its merits, especially when we got a few years older and started drinking, but for now though, we mostly hung out in the living quarters upstairs. In the first year of running *The Cricketers*, Hammys dad, Paul Snr, had opened the doors and welcomed in the local striking miners to use the pub as a base or meeting point. Their wives and families were also encouraged to drop by for free food, as these striking activists were determined to protect not just the future of their industry, but the welfare and livelihoods of their community. I hear a lot of propaganda and nonsense spoken about that period now, especially the miners. Thatcher's reign is almost glorified in certain media circles. If people had witnessed first-hand the impact her government had upon towns like ours, then I don't think they would be so quick to celebrate her vision of a Greater Britain. Not only did she dismantle our industries, she also divided and destroyed the working classes of our country, and those drastic societal changes have proved both damaging and irreversible.

Our music tuned into the political climate too; we had something to rally against, there was always a protest gig to attend back then, and some of the most memorable gigs I have seen were at a benefit or rally of some sort. Billy Bragg, or The Redskins on the same bill as Ted Hawkins. Or *Red Wedge*, which fused together artists as diverse as Morrissey and Marr, Gary Kemp, Jimmy Ruffin and The Communards as well as The Style Council, Madness, Lloyd Cole and Tom Robinson.

I had a lot of fun hanging out at *the Cricks*. It had a kind of novelty value that never really wore off, and loads of characters would frequent the place on a daily basis. In Atherstone everyone is known by another name or nickname, which usually bears absolutely no resemblance to their actual birth name. I know such people as Pudding, Chicken, Mushy, Radish, Soggy, Eggy, Squirmal, Hoss, Peanut, Sage, Cocoa, Sparrow, Custard, Spud, Potato Yed, Kidney, Pigeon, Rocket, Rabbit, Pup, Cow Head, Wagger, Dabber, Grubby, Tibby, Doddy, Dodder, Fodder, Cocky, Rocky, Babby, Shady, Dragon, Wizard, Roadrunner, Tippy, Cakey and Artic Roll. Even Dick Cheshire, the bloke who had arranged that visit to *Keresley Pit* was known as Dry Batch! We ourselves followed suit and kept the tradition by referring to Phil our drummer as Tates or Taters, because one of his ancestors apparently made crisps. His own father had the moniker of "Tuff" Ford (what's round and brown all year round? Tuffy Taters crisps!) It's a funny old place my hometown, and it was during this time at the pub that I became more familiar with its marvellous quirks and peculiarities.

Once Hammy had cemented his enduring friendship with me, he virtually stopped buying records, and just listened to mine. We moved as a unit, had exactly the same tastes, we would discover things together, and we barely spent a single day apart anyway, so Hammy figured we only needed one collection between us, and already it was obvious that I'd got the bug for accumulating and hoarding stuff. I had still held on to my toys and comics from my childhood, so what difference would a few thousand LP's make? As immaculately turned-out as Hammy usually was, he didn't give the same care and attention to the records as I would, so around the time of him moving into *the Cricks*, I had to put a ban on him borrowing my LPs for any prolonged amount of time. He spent most of his teenage years sat in front of my stereo at my mum and dad's anyway, what was mine was his, but he knew they wouldn't last five minutes languishing at his place. I turned up one Sunday morning to find the sleeve of my *Too Rye-Aye* LP by Dexys positioned neatly against the radiator. Thankfully, the heating hadn't been required so the actual vinyl inside was warp-free, but where was my inner sleeve? Hammy was quite apologetic, and inquired immediately. Ita, his mum, came to the rescue – "Oh Sheas", she said in her soft Irish accent, "I thought it would be yours, and our Paul left it out last night, so I put it somewhere safe ... Here you go, I've folded it up all nice and neat for you". She handed me back my missing inner sleeve for *Too Rye-Aye*, which had now shrunk from twelve-inch size to a compact four-inch tiny square. It did however fold out to make a lovely creased six-square effect. Hammy had his head in his hands. What could I do but laugh? I still have it actually, and I'm pleased I do.

Hammy himself did not fare much better. I arrived one Christmas Day morning to find him still in bed. I had bought him Elvis Costello's new album *Punch The Clock* and passed it to him to open, all neatly-wrapped in Christmas paper, the album inside pristine and still shrink-wrapped straight from the shop. "Fuck me youth, you're not gonna believe this", said Hammy, "I've got you exactly the same album! ... Nice one mate", he continued as he took the gift from me and started to unwrap his LP. "Oh, there's yours mate, on the stereo, I ain't had time to wrap it yet, I was playing it last night to check it out, great album eh, Sheas?" I looked across at the stereo to see the record still on the turntable, and the sleeve propped up next to it (thankfully the inner hadn't been redesigned by Ita just yet). I ended up seizing the sealed one back from Hammy's clutches, and made him keep the copy he'd been enjoying. Of course we both just laughed. Typical Hammy.

After the debacle and fiasco surrounding our first experience of a recording studio, my disappointment and frustration must have been obvious and apparent to all around me. My dad certainly picked up on it. The recording wasn't cheap either, it had cost us a few hundred quid, and I had to tap him up to subsidise my share of the bill. I was gutted to have to fork out for something that none of us was remotely happy with. My parents, especially my dad, knew that by now this wasn't some overnight fad or pastime. We were quite serious, committed and dedicated to making this whole band thing work. Rather than let us get ripped off or make bad decisions again, he decided that maybe he should take a bit more of a vested interest, cast a watchful eye over proceedings, and maybe help us develop. I didn't mind him looking after us as long as the other lads had no objections, and he stated right from the off that the music was our department, he would give no opinion on that, his role would be to promote it, get us better gigs, and more than anything steer us right so we wouldn't get shafted again. We were left to concentrate solely on the music.

The first task he accomplished with relative ease was finding us a couple of horn players, Stavros and Pablo to you, with their real names, Guy Greenway and Paul Tunicliffe, becoming redundant the moment they stepped into the rehearsal room with us (we are from Atherstone remember, plus we already had one Paul in the band). Stav played trumpet, Pablo tenor saxophone; it was just the addition we'd been looking for to re-ignite that organic soul vibe that we were attempting to achieve. It always had to be a big band. Horns and keys were as vital as bass and drums. We rehearsed hard, and word started to spread on the local scene that we were almost ready for business.

Around the same time, a few of the best bands in our area were in turmoil and transition. Mark Mortimer's band The Dream Factory were no exception. They had experienced a little taste of success, a couple of single releases on Neil Rushton's credible *Inferno* label, and even a full page feature in national rock weekly *Sounds*, but progress had begun to stall, and they were struggling to appeal beyond their faithful scooterist crowd, which frustrated their ambitious alto sax player Andy Codling.

We were close with the Factory boys, and they had been good to us, especially Mark, giving us gigs and name-dropping us in the press. I thought they were a great band; their gigs were always an event in those formative years, real exciting affairs and always packed to the rafters. I just thought they had to be patient and bide their time, and widespread recognition would surely land at their door. So, I was somewhat surprised and taken aback when their sax player showed an interest in defecting over to our camp, expressing his desire to join Dance Stance. It was a real big thing for us at the time, a compliment too, but I was wary of treading on Mark's toes, as he had been instrumental in getting us up and running and playing in front of our first audiences. I wasn't privy to the indoor politics going on behind the scenes with The Dream Factory, but Hammy and I had got to know Andy Codling quite well by now. He was a shy character, fairly reserved, but seemed to open up in our company. He was much older than us, our senior by almost 10 years, and he grew up listening to jazz, Steely Dan, Rickie Lee Jones and Tom Waits. It was a world that could feed our musical fascination. We were interested in him, and we just seemed to connect. We'd be at parties after gigs and I'd be as interested in what Coddy had been listening to as I would in what girls were knocking about. He'd tell me about a Was (not Was) album which featured Mel Tormé singing a torch ballad. I was intrigued by his knowledge and wisdom, we could learn from Coddy, and I liked hanging out with him. He always had a drink too. If you were at someone's house and the beer had been caned, Coddy always had a spare stash hidden away. He seemed to pull them out from underneath his hat, just magic his own bar up at will. We weren't complaining anyway. I think we left it to old Ray (my dad) to thrash out the transfer details, but within a month or two Coddy had clocked off at the Factory for good, and was now a full-time member of Dance Stance and writing our brass arrangements.

The other local stalwarts to hit the skids around the same time were a band called Love On Board, who were heavily influenced by the *Postcard Rec*ords bands, or *The young sound of Scotland* as it was sometimes referred to. Bands such as Orange Juice, The Fire Engines, Josef K, Friends Again, a kind of jangly indie pop hybrid. Love On Board were a tremendous band, a real tight unit of friends who appeared to have enormous amounts of fun making music together. Their gigs could be chaotic, beautiful and shambolic in equal parts, certainly unpredictable but always inspirational. Unlike us, they recorded their first demos in a glorified shed, copying tapes themselves from the cheapest cassettes they could find from their local petrol station to sell at their gigs, and it sounded fucking brilliant.

Their guitarist was the best, totally unique. Most kids pick up a guitar and play the bog- standard clichéd rock riffs of Led Zeppelin or Deep Purple. Nick Read couldn't have been further removed from that, he really stood apart. His first gig was seeing The Ramones at Birmingham Odeon, where he had stormed the stage to pogo about in his youthful exuberance. He had listened to his father's country records and Shadows LPs, and he was more a mash of James Burton and Tom Verlaine when I first met him. His playing was killer, and he was still only 19 years old. Nick looked great too, totally different to us at first, but he looked like a pop star already. For a start, he was hipster thin, plus he was tall, his raven-haired quiff piled high, with a single strand dropping over his eye. He carried no weight at all, probably not helped by the fact that around the time I first met Nick he had just been released from hospital, after being involved in a near fatal car smash. I think he'd been on a drip-feed for a while, which just exaggerated his rake-like features, but his striking rock 'n' roll physique was there naturally too, and he both epitomised and exuded cool. He was one funny fucker too; in fact, all those Love On Board dudes were. Glenn Lewis, Neil Jones and John Twist, they were a good combination, always upbeat and laughing, good to be around. I was not only astonished when they called it a day and broke the band up, I was devastated too, as a fan of their music. I knew we would have to move quickly if we wanted to get Nick Read involved with our band. A talent like his at the time wasn't going to hang around too long. Of course, we already had one guitarist, with Dave in the band, but I knew Nick was more of a lead guitarist and Dave's forte was chopping out and funkin' up rhythms, so I figured the two would make a happy marriage working together. I felt I had to act upon this opportunity regardless. I called Nick up and asked what he planned to do now Love On Board were no more, and did he fancy coming to rehearse with us? He did, why not? Let's see how it goes. It went perfectly, hand in glove, the sun was indeed starting to shine out of our behinds, as the song goes.

We were now a nine-piece band. We had our own little orchestra, the sound Hammy and I envisaged in our heads was starting to come to fruition, and with my dad overseeing the ball-ache of getting gigs, organising vans etc., and generally taking care of business, this would be the real beginning of Dance Stance mark one. I still had no idea what

I wanted to do now I had left school though, fannying about at college and hiding from the world was all well and good, but I needed to earn some money. I needed a job.

7 – IF JOHNNY HATES JAZZ, THEN I HATE JOHNNY

I was using college as some sort of safe-haven where I could take cover from the outside world and consider my options. I can't deny that I had a good time there, and met some great people, but I was restless, and frustrated by not really knowing what I wanted to do with myself in the long term. I was determined to not get caught up in factory work, or the nine-to-five suicide, where you end up wishing away the hours and days. In whatever role I was to secure employment, I wanted to make sure that I enjoyed it rather than endured it. The college was based in Nuneaton, and almost every day I would wander into town and check out the record shops. As well as two independents (*Shooting Star* in Heron Way, and a tiny but busy shop on Dugdale Street called *What Records*), there was *Taylors*, the local TV and hi-fi shop, who had a record department in the back of their store, as well as *Woolworths* and *WH Smiths*. I was mostly interested in the indies, as they specialized in and stocked up on all the weird and wonderful stuff that was more to my taste. You'd strike up a rapport with the staff in the independent shops, they would get to know the sort of stuff you'd usually buy, and maybe also turn you on to a new thing or two.

What Records' Dave Smith was certainly good for this. He would happily share his impressive knowledge of music, and despite being older and from a different background, he wasn't patronising, and nor did he give it all the "it was better in my day" bollocks. He had seen some of the greats too, and I think he took a shine to me, as he could tell that I was genuinely interested in hearing what Marvin Gaye or The Temptations would have been like to witness. Similarly, he wanted to hear the buzz I was getting from Dexys gigs or from seeing The Jam. I popped in to see him most days, and to study form amongst the racks. During one of these visits, he dropped a couple of questions on me; what was I up to, and had my college course finished yet? Tim, the owner of the shop, was expanding his business, opening new shops elsewhere, and so they needed to take someone on full-time to help Dave out in the Nuneaton shop. How was I fixed, and did I fancy it? I was just a year in to what was meant to be a two-year college course. But fuck all that! This was the opportunity I had been looking for, and I was ready to leave at the drop of a hat! Me? Working in a record shop? Kid in a sweet shop! When can I start?

The interview was just a formality, no CV required, just come and meet the boss, have a chat, and they would work the terms of my employment out from there. I'd only really met Tim Ellis a couple of times before, as he mainly let Dave handle the day-to-day running of the shop, especially now that he was spreading his wings and expanding his business. Dave had recommended me and put me forward for the job, saying he thought I would be the perfect candidate, but I'm not sure Tim was quite so convinced. I think he would have preferred a young, attractive female behind the counter, but as I'd later find out, it took a long time to convince Tim about anyone's personality. He was fairly guarded, something of a closed book, and I think he thought the worst of anyone before he got to know them. It was just as well then, that on the day of my interview I had a real bad case of glandular fever. Having virtually no voice to speak of or with, I was unable to fuck up my interview.

I started work the day before my eighteenth birthday; Tuesday 15th October 1985. At £25 a week, on the *YTS* (*Youth Training Scheme*), I was kind of on trial for 6 months. Loving it immediately, as I knew I would, I quickly immersed myself in the over-the-counter culture. It was an interesting time to begin working in a record shop, as radical changes were afoot. I started just prior to the CD boom and the introduction of digital technology, a revolution that had punters buying their old record collections all over again. Records shifted in numbers back then, and business was healthy. It was clear to see why Tim was able to develop his empire. During that first week, I remember a new release being Iron Maiden's *Live After Death*; we had boxes and boxes of them everywhere, and we were literally tripping over them. I recall thinking to myself that we were never going to sell all of these, and yet by the Thursday we had to re-order. I was astounded by how many LPs were sold. If there were a big release on a Monday, folks would be queuing at the door, waiting for the shop to open at 9 a.m.

There was never a dull moment. On Mondays, all the new releases would arrive to be sorted and put out in the racks, plus you would have to change the top 40 chart wall around for that week. Tuesdays we would get all the re-stocks for what we had sold over the weekend. Wednesday was my day off, Thursdays we would be swamped by DJs, looking for new releases and chart fodder ready for their Double Deck

Disco action the forthcoming weekend. On Fridays, everything stepped up a gear, and we got really busy with punters, on top of which I'd still be tea-boy and errand-boy, but I didn't mind that. Saturdays were just total mayhem, and that small space would be crammed full, from 9 a.m. until we shut the doors at 5 p.m.

The only downside to taking on my new occupation was having to give up my football on a Saturday, both playing, and watching my beloved Leeds United. Dad had given up his season ticket at Coventry a couple of seasons previously; I don't think he ever got the same enjoyment from going once I'd grown up and no longer went to the games with him. I'd go and see Leeds with my mates, or older lads I knew who could drive, though Dad and I still attended the odd game together, even the Adders occasionally just for old times' sake. I didn't miss playing too much at the time. I started when I was eight with the local junior side Atherstone Rangers, so I'd had a good ten years at it, and played in some good sides. I had a (very brief) trial spell at Luton Town, which didn't work out, but more than anything, I'd really enjoyed playing in a team with the lads I grew up and went to school with. I had no real expectations of taking it any further, although I am quite surprised that some of the lads I played alongside didn't get scouted and turn pro. Some of them were easily good enough. It would be almost another ten years before I made a return to the football pitch and once again donned my *Puma Kings*.

Dave Smith, who managed the shop in Dugdale Street, was a great mentor in many ways. He had impeccable taste in music, and more than anyone I knew at that time, he opened up my ears to so many different things. Hearing all this fantastic music, while I was getting paid to be there, was an awakening. To an extent, I was still investigating my modernist and soul tendencies, searching back in order to move forwards, always discovering something exciting. But Dave was now giving me a daily lesson in the riches and wonders of music's bewildering history. Eight hours a day ... just imagine how much you can digest in a week. My head was buzzing! I got turned on to Little Feat, Graham Parker and the Rumour, Neil Young, Nick Drake, Joni Mitchell: so much stuff. It blew my mind. Dave handed me a cassette one day and suggested I should check it out. It was a double live album of Van Morrison, recorded in 1973 with his eleven-piece band, who had the brilliant moniker *The Caledonia Soul Orchestra*. I had heard Van Morrison before of course, and I knew the big hits that he'd had with

Them and a few other bits. But I hadn't really taken that much notice, until now. Dave knew I loved Dexys, and obviously they had covered *Jackie Wilson Sai*d, but I hadn't really gone back to the source and checked Van out properly. The album was called *It's Too Late To Stop Now*. I didn't play much else for a month. I wore that cassette out. It was exactly what I had been looking for, the connection, the bridge between black American soul, r'n'b influences and what I'd been digging with Dexys. It was the best live album I had ever heard. No frills, just the sound of a band right at the top of their game, bringing Van's wonderful songs to life. I spent the majority of the next month's wages on Van Morrison's entire back catalogue. I had some catching up to do.

And so it was that a kind of pattern unfolded. By the very nature of my new job, I would get this marvellous opportunity to hear music in abundance; all types of stuff, from the varied and various genres of bygone eras, right through to the latest releases, promos of which we received by the score, left for us by the record company reps. Punters would ask to hear certain records sometimes too, either to check them out while they were browsing, or in some cases, to check for faults. I remember a bloke coming in once to return an album by John Martyn, called *Solid Air*, claiming that it jumped on the opening track. I offered him a replacement and suggested that we should probably give it a whirl on the decks to check it before he left, so he wouldn't have to trek down again to return another copy, as sometimes these little imperfections can affect the whole pressing. I dropped the needle onto side one, the title track. I had never heard John Martyn before, and by the look of him on other sleeves that I'd seen while straightening up the LPs in the 'M' section, I expected a traditional folky dullard. He had a beard for fuck's sake! And even worse, on a recent album of his I noticed that Phil Collins was listed as a guest musician. How much worse can it get? I braced myself. What I hadn't expected was the incredible, other worldly, stoned jazz vibe which came creeping out of the shop speakers, and then that slurred, charismatic, captivating voice. I was shocked. That was next month's wages fucked now too.

This was also the year that I finally passed my driving test, third time lucky, and so my errands started to run beyond just making tea and filing away records. Tim took full advantage of my wheels, and made me delivery boy, dropping and distributing stock between his new shops, one of which was situated in Coalville in Leicestershire, which when you've just started driving actually feels like it's situated at the end of the earth. It always rained when I went to Coalville, but I didn't mind this additional role, as it broke the days up sometimes, and I quite liked Bess, one of the girls who ran the Coalville shop. The other part of Tim's expansion included buying up the old *Carousel* record shop on Leicester Street in Bedworth. Bedworth was, and still is, a small market town situated about 5 miles from both Coventry and Nuneaton, with a population of just over 30,000. It reminds me very much of where I grew up in Atherstone. One main school, so everyone pretty much knows everyone else, far too many pubs for its size, and almost everyone you meet is welcoming and friendly. A real working-class community.

The lad who managed the shop at that time had been employed by the previous owners. He was a goth kid called Mark Richards, a young lad of a similar age to me. I really liked him, and when we worked together on the odd days I was sent over to help out, I really looked forward to it. Tim, however, had it in for Mark. Right from the start of his tenure as the new proprietor, he thought that Mark's goth image put people off coming into the shop. I thought that was just a flimsy excuse, but it was clear that Tim would replace Mark at the first opportunity. What I didn't realise was that I was being groomed as his replacement, hence why I found myself spending more and more time working over in Bedworth alongside Mark. Mine and Mark's musical tastes couldn't have been further apart, so far removed that at times it was comical. I'd be keen to check out the new Anita Baker album, while he'd work himself up into a frenzy over the new Alien Sex Fiend LP. We did, however, strike common ground over our infatuation for one artist, and together we attended what is still one the best gigs I have ever been to. Tom Waits at the Hammersmith Odeon on his *Frank's Wild Years* tour. Coddy (Dream Factory and Dance Stance) had mentioned Tom Waits before, but the name hadn't stuck then.

On Fridays, *Channel 4* screened *The Tube*, a music programme which showcased live bands. It was prime time TV too, showing from 5.30 p.m. until 7 p.m., not shoved out on the graveyard shift, and it really deserves much more credit for breaking a lot of new artists. Most Friday evenings, Hammy and I would meet on the corner of Friary Road, and head for a night around town, fueled by conversation of what and who had been featured on that week's edition of *The Tube*. On one of those nights out, neither of us could get our words out quick enough.

"Fucking hell, did you see that shit on *The Tube*? What the fuck was that all about? … Uncle Vernon …Uncle Vernon ... was it a piss take? It was fucking terrible!" We didn't shut up about it all night though, and the more pissed we got, so the words would alter: "Uncle Herman ... Uncle Herman …" We sang it all week. It was, of course, Tom Waits performing *Cemetery Polka* live, and a few weeks later we both surrendered and bought his album *Raindogs*, and to this day it remains one my favourite works of musical genius.

By 1987, at the age of twenty, I had the job of managing the Bedworth shop. As much as I felt sorry for Mark, and tried to defend him to Tim, I knew it was a fruitless exercise. His cards were marked and he was out, regardless of my interventions. I relished the responsibility, and took quite well to the task of establishing the shop. Business was good, and I even got a hike in wages after getting taken on full-time, no longer on my £25 *YTS* pittance. I quickly proved that I was more than capable of running things, and soon enough I was pretty much left to get on with it. Tim would only visit once, maybe twice a week, so in some ways it felt like my own little haven. It wasn't like work, and in fact I can't believe I used to get paid for it. The days were filled with such adventure, laughter and total unpredictability. I have never known a place attract so many misfits, oddballs and eccentrics, but above all they were fantastic characters, and I became the ringmaster, encouraging each and every one of them. If I was to spend eight and a half hours a day here, six days a week, then we were going to have some fun. Where Tim and I differed was that I thought a record shop should be like a hangout for the local music heads, a meeting place where people could talk about what they were listening to, who they had seen that week, turn others on to sounds, check out what was new, and take as much time as they needed to flick through the racks. Tim just wanted the money. In and out, no hanging about. This may be fine if you're located in a busy city centre, but we were in a tiny Warwickshire town. To keep customers coming back, I knew that we had to embrace the enthusiasts, the eccentrics and the obsessives, and not alienate them. I also loved talking to them, and considering the size of the town, we had scores of them come through the door.

Pet Shop Boy, for example, wasn't a nutter. Mildly unusual maybe, but certainly not a loon. In fact he became one of my closest friends at this period in my life, mainly because he came into the shop every single day from 1986 until the doors finally closed for good 10 years later in

1996. People thought he worked there. He worked the nightshift, loading Lorries on the local industrial estate, and then by day he'd spend his time in the shop. He wanted to see what would unfold, and something always did; he never left disappointed. I called him Pet Shop Boy because when I first met him he was crazy for them, buying everything in all formats. I couldn't stand them (still can't) but I admired the lad's commitment, even if I did take the piss a little. In those early days our musical tastes were polar opposites, but I think you bond over that addictive nature that comes with collecting records. I can identify with that. So, Pet Shop Boy became part of the furniture, fixtures and fittings. Needless to say, Tim hated him, even attempting to ban him from the shop on several occasions. But I just wouldn't have it; he was a local face, people liked him, I liked him and he bought custom into the shop. On the quiet days when I worked alone, he'd keep me company, and on days when we got hired help in, usually our Saturday girl in need of extra hours, we'd sod off and have a game of football in the park, or go over to the pub, or occasionally invent games on the rear car park, like Cowboys and Indians with cap-guns, or kite flying. In fact, I and the Pet Shop Boy were once in the middle of a fully-fledged battle on the car park, shooting each other with cap-guns, locked in warfare, when Tim pulled up in his car only to see me quickly dive under the wheel of a Ford Escort in a vain attempt to hide. I sheepishly came out and surrendered my toy weapon, taking the rap for playing imaginary gun-fighting instead of attending to the *Sony* returns. That was the first of many written warnings (by '96 I think I could have decorated my house with them).

There are hundreds of stories from this period, and many of the characters deserve their very own biography, but some of those I can recall immediately include the next few oddballs. First up, Cecil. Cecil was an OAP, probably in his mid to late seventies. There was a newsagent's next door, and Cecil was one of a few who occasionally wandered into our shop, shuffling the full forty yards down to the counter, stopping halfway to regain his breath, and asking, at the end of the mammoth journey, for twenty *B&H* and a *Daily Mirror*. After about the third or fourth time of telling Cecil that he was in the record shop and not the newsagent's (I used to let him and the other wanderers do the walk), he asked me if I had a record – *Sheila* by Tommy Roe. I did, and then Cecil became a regular. Cecil's thing was 50's Rock 'n' Roll and Sixties pop, so if he saw an ad on TV for a compilation that he fancied, he'd ring me up to see if we had it for him. The main problem with this was that Cecil had the worst stutter known to man, and once he got into the habit of buying records off me, he'd always, without fail, ring me first. But Cecil didn't have a phone at home, so he'd use the nearest phone box. I'd answer the phone. "Hello, *What Records*". Beep, beep, beep … The coin would drop and a voice would say "O-oo-oo-o D-d-d-d D-d You u-u y-y-oo n-n-n-n-n-n-n-n- …….You know who this is d-d-d-d-d-don't you?" I did, obviously. "No. Who is it please" I would reply.

"It it it's s-s-s-s-s i-i-i-i It's Cec-c-cil" Beeeeeeep. The money would run out.

He'd ring again, and we'd go through all that again for about another ten minutes before he'd finally get to what it was he wanted. Then he would get me to read out all the tracks that featured on the LP. So I would say "Side one, you've got *Reelin' and Rockin'* by Chuck Berry". He would always repeat it - " Oooooo-ahhh Y-y-y yes, Ch-ch-ch-Chuck B-b-b-b-Berry, g-g-g-g-good - "R-r-r-r- ..."

Reelin' and Rockin, I would interject.

"Oooooooo-ahhh Y-y-y-yes R-r-r-r-…"

I think old Cecil spent more money in the payphone than what the actual album itself cost him.

Then there was Pinhead and Parrot, who always taped the top 40 on a Sunday, and would come in on the Monday and buy a load of 7" singles. Pinhead and Parrot were a mother and daughter combination. The daughter had a disproportionately small head for her rather wide frame, and the mother always repeated everything that the daughter said, hence my rather unflattering choice of nickname for them.

"We've taped the pops", Pinhead would declare.

"Taped the Pops", came the echo from Parrot.

"Mel & Kim's a good un'", shouts Pinhead.

"Mel & Kim's a good un'", shouts Parrot.

"Seen it on the pops", Pinhead tells me.

"Seen it on the pops", confirms Parrot.

They always bought me chocolates at Christmas. They would wrap them up, but I knew it was a box of chocolates. A lovely, kind gesture, but for some reason I could never bring myself to eat them. I got it into my head that they'd won them the previous year on a raffle, or at bingo, and then passed them on to me. I'm not sure why, as they were always in date. It was probably more due to the fact that the mother, Parrot, always had a faint whiff of wee about her. Maybe she was just excited about the new Mel & Kim offering. I shouldn't have really let it come between me and a box of *Milk Tray*.

Mrs. Harris, aka Hot Dog Harris. She never knew who the song was by, or what the song was called, and always misheard it. "Have you got that song *The Farmer*? I don't know who sings it, but it's definitely called *The Farmer* - It's in the charts". I go through the whole top 75, but there's no reference to any farmers whatsoever. I even mention The Farmer's Boys on the off chance that Hot Dog has been checking out Norwich's finest indie pop merchants.

"I'll sing it", she offers. *The Farmer ... a-licky boom boom down ...The Farmer.*

INFORMER! You berk!", I tell her, referring to Snow's 1992 hit.

Mrs Harris picked up the 'Hot Dog' addition to her name as she used to wear these sort of padded coats with really loud swirling patterns on, the sort that would be impossible to buy anywhere should the unlikely need take you, and she always pushed along one of those tartan shopping trolleys, but she absolutely stank of hot dogs and onions every single time she came in the shop. God only knows what her house was like; maybe she had a bonfire and BBQ every day?

Thursday was DJ day. Word had spread about my unorthodox approach, and we had started to attract a lot of DJs, not just from Bedworth, but also Coventry, Nuneaton and other surrounding areas. By Thursday afternoon I'd have accumulated and stocked up on all the new releases for the week, and also had promos galore that various reps would drop in free of charge. The DJs would clamour to get hold of these upfront, so I made Thursday afternoons the time when I'd get them all to congregate in the shop, and I'd spin all the latest releases and promos, and have them fighting over who was having what. In reality I usually had enough copies to go round, but I'd make then sweat, and so rack up the sales. Some weeks we'd have up to twenty DJs all gathered in the shop, eager for that week's tunes. It was really comical to hear their banter, all bullshitting each other about what they were doing, how much they were earning, what clubs they were playing and so on. They were all eccentrics too, the mobile disco brigade. We had Pepperbox, who prided himself on having every record in the top 40. Every week, he bought everything that charted, and always insisted that he had a remote-control disco. Then there was Demon Derek, who also distributed dodgy porn films to the other DJs, and swapped them up every Thursday; Dancing Danny, a Jamaican who would tell the worst jokes ever; Get Down Shep, a real boring fella who was the spitting image of John Noakes from *Blue Peter*; Pepsi Man who plied us with free cans of pop, maybe to try and get a bit of extra discount; Plug, who looked like the character from the *Bash Street Kids*; Big John from Chapel End, who used to break out unannounced into impressions of various characters from *Wacky Races*, which was fairly bizarre to say the least. We also had Eurovision Man, who only appeared twice a year, just before the *Eurovision Song Contest* and then again just after. He was a strange bloke with *NHS* glasses (before they became fashionable). He also sported a ginger beard and a quarter-length tweed jacket, with a plastic bag constantly tucked under his arm. Then there was Ollie, who looked like Lon Chaney, and called himself DJ Breakfast, and would dress up as Tina Turner. He was way out there. A real young kid used to drop by after school in his uniform, always asking for the most obscure and hip Indie records, almost like he'd swallowed the pages of the *NME* which he always clutched under his arm. I liked him, of course, but I did think at times he was making names up just to try and catch me out. He never smiled though, always completely deadpan. Then one day he just disappeared. Apparently, his dad was in the Army, so the young lad was often uprooted and had to move to another town and school. The next time I saw him was actually on the cover of the *NME* that he once so worshipped. His name was Pete. Pete Doherty.

The Record company reps loved the atmosphere of the place too, and many dropped in at least twice a week, just to hang out as well as do some business. They looked after me, I looked after them, but more than anything it was a place for everyone to meet. We started a football league on Tuesdays, which again took place in the shop car park out the back. Me, Pet Shop Boy and a few regulars would play reps from *Warner Brothers*, *Polygram*, *RCA*, *Pinnacle*, *EMI* and *Virgin* every Tuesday afternoon. Grown men chasing each other about, dripping with sweat on a car park in the middle of the afternoon. Most of the reps had other calls to go on to in Coventry or Leicester, and would arrive stinking and sweating from our matches.

In those days the record company reps would sometimes bring artists or bands out on the road with them to visit shops, to see how things work on the shop floor and maybe sign a few copies of their latest release, to help with PR and sales. Many would drop by on me, and most I found to be really amicable and we'd get on fine. One time around 1988 though, we got a visit from Calvin Hayes, son of the late Mickie Most, and at that time one third of the successful chart pop group Johnny Hates Jazz, who'd just scored a couple of big hits in the UK. His ego could barely get through the door, and we instantly got off on the wrong footing. But out of respect to my *Virgin Records* rep, who was a good friend, I attempted to keep things as amicable and as comfortable as possible. Obviously, I didn't let on that I thought they were a complete pile of shite. I feign interest in his group and ask how it's all been going, and how the current tour is doing, but he doesn't want to know me. He's too busy trying to tap up the female staff, and when our young girl offers him a tea or coffee, he says "Oh darling, have you any champagne?" You're in Johnny Hates Jazz mate, you're not Bryan Ferry. I leave him to his vain attempts to romance our young female staff, who are looking at me to save them from his over-zealous, hands-on approach. I decide to make him that coffee as an olive branch, a peace offering. Only instead of filling up the kettle in the kitchen, I decide to fill it up myself in the toilet, taking some consolation and comfort in the fact that Champagne Calvin is sipping on a lovely mixture of *Nescafe* and urine, whilst attaching himself to our Kate the Saturday girl.

I truly did love my job. I looked forward to getting up in the morning and going to work. You really never knew what adventure or escapade would unfold. It also afforded me the time to pursue my band activities. In fact the two worked hand in hand, as Tim decided to set up a record label, and one of the first things he thought about releasing, to capitalize on the unmistakable growing interest in the band, was a single by Dance Stance.

8 – LET'S GO TO JERSEY

"Maybe we should ask in the post office", suggested Hammy, in all his infinite wisdom. We were on a mission, a search, like two detectives hunting for clues. Our investigations had taken us all the way, on foot I hasten to add, to the village of Polesworth. What, or more to the point who, were we trying to track down? We'd heard an unconfirmed whisper that a bona fide ex-member of Dexys Midnight Runners was living locally. The word, as flimsy as we had it, was that he was living in Polesworth (which was already home to soul legend Edwin Starr, so anything was possible), and it was rumoured that he was setting up a recording studio, and maybe looking to work with local bands. This was too good an opportunity to miss out on, we thought. Hammy could talk me into practically anything; he had a perfect charm about him, he could dress any potential situation or proposed adventure to sound like it was something that we couldn't possibly miss out on, and that included embarking upon a wild goose chase, walking five miles up the canal towpath all the way to Polesworth village on a freezing afternoon, to ask a bemused old lady behind the village Post Office counter if she knew where Paul Speare, ex-sax player with Dexys Midnight Runners lived ... "He played on the *Too-Rye-Ay* album", Hammy offered, trying to jog the baffled pensioner's memory banks. Our pursuit was in vain. We did, however, get some scant consolation over a pint in the village pub, where the landlord told us that a tall fellow had recently moved into the area who used to play in a band that were quite famous, but wasn't sure where he lived, maybe Pooley View estate? So we trekked around the houses. I'm really not sure what we were looking for as a signal. Maybe we thought that we would see torn denim dungarees hanging out on a washing line. It was time for Plan B (no pun intended).

My dad had taken to his Brian Epstein role quite well, and for our part, we had knocked ourselves into shape, and were starting to sound accomplished beyond our years, buoyed on by the introduction of the horns and Nick Read's presence. We thought it wise to bat the task of super-sleuth over to Ray, and needless to say Paul Speare was in attendance at our next local gig, which was at the Rathole in Tamworth. He liked what he saw, and it is fair to say that we hit it off with him right from the start. He understood us, and he made the obvious and perfect choice to oversee and produce our next foray into the recording studio. This time around, we considered our options a little more thoughtfully, and we settled upon using *Rich Bitch Studios* in Birmingham, where we would attempt to record our debut single, which my boss Tim at the record shop proposed to release on his *What Records* label. With Paul at the helm, and more members to consider this time around, the sessions were organised with almost military precision. I would go in and record the rhythm track with Phil, Nick and Dave, then Dick would add keyboards on a separate session, the horns worked through the night shift, and Hammy added vocals on top. It felt like a proper recording session, as if we were actually making a record, and creating something.

We completed two songs (A and B-side) over the course of a few days. The other band that were always leaving the studio as we arrived were Birmingham's all-girl indie group We've Got A Fuzzbox And We're Going To Use It. They were recording their debut album at the same time. Our single *The Other Side of Paradise* got released on 7" vinyl that summer. We only pressed about a thousand copies, and it sold well locally, and brought us a bit more attention. It sounds dreadfully dated now of course, but it served its purpose, and we were moving in the right direction. With the wind in our young sails, momentum and interest were steadily growing. We'd started out playing in youth clubs and staging our own gigs at local Working Men's clubs, and within six months of my dad taking over the band's affairs, we were playing at universities and polytechnics all over the country, securing credible support slots along the way to the likes of Geno Washington, Steve Harley, The Jazz Defectors, Hazel O'Connor and more. We even got riders, with *Nottingham Trent Polytechnic* being the very first venue where we experienced this remarkable act of goodwill. We couldn't believe our eyes - masses of free food laid out on a table, pizza, sandwiches, crisps, even cake. Towels and water had been laid out for us, but of course, we could hardly contain our excitement to find several crates of beer stacked in the corner of our dressing room, readily available for consumption. This Rock 'n' Roll malarkey was becoming more attractive by the hour! Certainly better than a night out round town, I could now go away to a different city most weekends with a minibus full of my best mates, play an hour's worth of music to packed university crowds full of kids the same age as us (which was an important thing to experience), then get pissed on free beer afterwards ... oh, and sometimes, we even got paid for it too!

Hammy wasn't the biggest of drinkers, beer wasn't really his thing. He enjoyed a tipple of *Jack Daniels* and *Coke*, but obviously, you can't knock that back 24/7 unless you have the consumption capabilities of Keith Richards. He began to get curious about alternative ways to get his kicks. A few years previously, when we had started attending gigs regularly, his senses would perk up when the aroma of marijuana smoke wafted through the hall. We went to see Curtis Mayfield at *Leicester University*, and roots reggae band Black Uhuru were supporting, which attracted a large contingent of Rastas to the gig, who proceeded to turn the air thick with ganja smoke, so much so that Hammy and I thought we were stoned just on the passive intake alone. This high certainly intrigued Hammy, and he started to experiment with it in the confines of his bedroom above the pub. I knew things were changing when Elvis Costello was being replaced on his turntable by Santana. He had a little pipe at first, and inhaled it that way, but very soon he became proficient in rolling up joints.

My first experience of his new-found passion for pot was one Wednesday afternoon on a day off from the record shop. He cajoled me into sharing a spliff with him. Now, I had not even smoked a cigarette before, it just didn't appeal to me, but as always, Hammy's persuasive nature convinced me that getting high on a Wednesday lunchtime in Atherstone would be the perfect and most natural way to while away a few hours. What he didn't tell me was that I would turn into a paranoid mess, develop an appetite the size of a small country, and not be able to string a cohesive sentence together for the rest of the day. I insisted that we walk out into town so I could buy some food. Hammy advised me to relax; suggesting that going out would be a bad move. I persisted, however; I had to move, I felt a weight coming on my shoulders. We had only just made it down Market Street and on to Long Street when I bumped into Mrs. Billingham, the mother of Gaz, a good friend of mine, who knew my family – "Hello Neil," she greeted me, "How's your mum and dad? I haven't seen them for a while. Are they OK?"
Now, Mrs. B might as well have been asking me about how the pound was shaping up against the dollar in the current economic climate. It feels like the light around me has dimmed, and a spotlight has fallen onto me. I hear the *Mastermind* theme music in my brain ... How were my mum and dad? Were they OK? I had no idea. I just stood there grinning back at her for what seemed like a fucking age, running that question over and over again in my head. How are my mum and dad? It doesn't even make sense. Are they OK? I don't know. So there I am,

stood outside *Supercigs* in the middle of Long Street, stoned out of my mind, clutching at least eight bags of crisps, and contemplating Mrs. Billingham's enquiry. I glance over to Hammy for help, but he has tears of laughter welling up in his eyes. I can't look at him, and finally I splutter out my answer ... "I'm not sure", and with that erratic reply, I kind of walk sideways back up Market Street, and return to the shelter of Hammy's bedroom.

I would come to experience a few more false starts and bouts of paranoia before I could actually tolerate inhaling weed at all, smoking has just never been my thing but Hammy took to it like a duck to water. It became his food, and to be fair it suited him. He could operate perfectly normally under its influence, whereas I would turn into a jabbering mess. Different strokes for different folks and all that, but now that Hammy was a convert, a smoke was always at hand if so desired. It wasn't always without complication though. The band had been booked to play in Jersey, over in the Channel Islands. In fact, we made two trips over there to perform, and perform we did. It was like we'd been let out on day release, and as was often the case, the music seemed to take a back seat to us having ourselves the best time we possibly could. Our first visit, in 1987, was high-spirited but fairly innocent, just what you'd expect from a gang of young lads let loose on a free weekend away, with just an hour's work to do over the course of three days. *The Tourist Board* had brought us over to play a concert in St. Helier's Howard Davis Park, and they had put us up in a top hotel, complete with a swimming pool and so on. It was really a family place, so they must have been horrified to see us turn up en masse.

Paul Speare had become almost part of our set up by now. He had opened a studio in Tamworth called *The Expresso Bongo*, and Dance Stance were regulars. I think he anticipated our sessions with a mixture of excitement and trepidation. Our determination to turn everything into one big party made Paul's task of actually getting our songs recorded something of a challenge. Hammy would begin every session with the ritual of tying a bandana around Paul's head, to awaken his "soul music production attributes". We must have almost bankrolled the place for a few years, so often did we frequent it to record demos of our songs, which were thankfully starting to come to us in abundance.

It was on our second trip to the fair island of Jersey that chaos ensued. By this time (1988), we had undergone yet another line-up change, which is somewhat the nature of the beast when you decide upon using a sizeable number of band members. The Delaney brothers had exited, and in came Simon "Chico" Hall on trombone and Richard Ward on keyboards. Richard was certainly a one-off; he was from Rugby, or as he liked to say, "Raag-bee" (he reckons its best pronounced half-Cockney and half-Brummie). I found him demonstrating *Kurzweil* organs in a shopping centre in Leicester. He could certainly play, but it was more his eccentricities that endeared him to the band. He picked up the moniker Lekiki, as he carried a keyring bearing that inscription. When we questioned him about what it meant, he said it was Hawaiian for Richard. Of course, he had never been anywhere near Hawaii. He was a speed freak too, not the drug, but at the wheel of a car. You really were putting your life on the line when you sat in the passenger seat with Lekiki. He'd drive on motorways stood up, with his head out of the sunroof. He did a handbrake turn on the M1 down to London once, with me in the car, ending up facing the wrong way, with traffic bearing down at us. He thought it was hilarious, and he was crying with laughter. He bought a battered old Fiat *Panda*, just because he thought it would make us laugh. I remember playing a gig up at *Sheffield University*, and Pablo had drawn the short straw and had to travel up with him. They arrived about an hour late, both of their faces soaked with rain, drenched top halves, but dry from the chest down. Lekiki had travelled up through a fierce rainstorm in his Fiat Panda, he'd turned the windscreen wipers up full to clear the torrential rain hitting the screen, and they'd flown off, so he had driven the majority of the journey with his head out of the window to see where he was going. He sensed no danger in this, he thought it was brilliant. Richard had a thing for S&M too, and he'd buy these magazines that looked more like a *Blake's 7* annual than a porn mag; you didn't see any flesh, just leather costumes, akin to something from a b-movie sci-fi flick. It kept him quiet for a while though. Anyway, I digress.

It was the summer of 1988, and we had been re-booked to play over in the Channel Islands at St. Helier's *Howard Davis Park*. Nine of us in the band, plus my dad and Paul Speare flew from Birmingham, while our two roadies Emo and Ceddy took the van full of our equipment over on the ferry. From the off it seemed like our trip was ill-fated; the plane was delayed, and the only real attraction in the airport's waiting lounge was the bar. So, after consuming beer like it was going to run out, and then continuing to quench our insatiable thirst whilst aboard the plane, we were all fairly well tanked-up by the time we landed in

Jersey. We staggered through an empty customs corridor humming an adapted version of an Ian Dury classic. Our take was "Sex & Drugs & Sausage Rolls". Before we knew it, we were besieged by Customs Officers, who sprang out from nowhere, more than eager to search us all. I knew we were clean, so had nothing to really be concerned about, none of the lads were daft enough to travel loaded up with gear. I knew that there was a lump of draw as big as a house brick concealed in the van that was coming across on the ferry, but we carried nothing over on the flight, so there was no cause for alarm. At least that's what I thought until I caught sight of one of the lad's face who was being frisked down by the authorities, I clocked that his expression changed as soon as they started fishing in the inside pocket of a waistcoat that was in his case. He'd left a load of amphetamine in there from a previous night out, and that was all they needed. They had also found Hammy's pipe and checked the gauze, they knew we were in a band, so now they asked how was the equipment getting across? We could not lie. They strip-searched the rest of us, pulled us into custody, and phoned the ferry port to stop our van on arrival.

I would like to have been a fly on the wall for the scene that unfolded down at the docks when our van rolled in. Ceddy, who was 6ft 7inches and covered in tattoos, was completely oblivious to the fact that he was driving a van not only full of our equipment, but also the week's drug stash. Emo, for his part, has been entrusted with the task of looking after the sizable chunk of smoke that we're bringing over the English Channel, and he doesn't flinch when customs single out the van and pull it over on entering St. Helier's docks. It takes the officers all of one minute to remove a panel at the foot of Emo's seat, and to locate our chunk of smoke. Ceddy, who feels like an extra on the set of Midnight Express, looks on in disbelief as Emo grabs the block of draw and throws it to the ground in complete denial – "I don't fucking believe this", cries Emo, "We've been set up!"

"No need for the charade son", says the customs officer. "We've got your band banged up at the airport".

Eventually, back at the airport, we're allowed to board a coach that will take us to our hotel. Hammy has his pipe confiscated and is let off. The lad with the whizz however has to remain in custody for a while longer. My dad stays with him at the airport, and also has to liaise with the authorities at the docks about getting Emo released, and our van actually into Jersey. The uncertainty of the consequences of all of this sobers our mood somewhat, and we check into our hotel (which is even plusher than the previous year) and await news.

It was late into the evening before my dad returned with both the boys who were detained in tow. To be fair, I don't think my dad had a fucking clue what was going on; it looked like it had aged him by a decade, and he was already suffering from heart complaints by this time, so it was probably the last thing he needed, but he gathered us all together on the balcony of the hotel's bar, and told us the news that two of our crew had been arrested for possession of drugs, and had been released, with court cases pending. He suggested that we keep it between ourselves and never mention it again, and reminded us that we were here to do a job, and that the engagement still stood. He'd seen quite enough for one day, and was ready to retire to the comfort of his bed for the night. It was time to forget about it and put it all behind us, and his parting shot to us all was – "There's a nightclub in the basement of the hotel, now go down there, have a few drinks, enjoy yourselves and forget about it – see you in the morning."

We got the keys to the van, and went to fetch the wraps of speed buried inside a flight case that the sniffer dogs hadn't traced. Lekiki tracked down the nearest sex shop to purchase some poppers (*amyl nitrate*) to snort, and Stav ordered every cocktail on the hotel's menu. By midnight, we were all completely battered again. The DJ in the nightclub got wind that there was a band staying in the hotel, and made a bit of a fuss of it, which in turn got the attention of a few girls down there, and before we know it, we somehow find ourselves at a party in a hotel room, with a load of beautiful young girls, all (literally) falling at our feet. I'm not sure who they thought we were, Curiosity Killed The Cat?

Next morning, on the way down to breakfast, I will never forget the sight of the cleaner lifting Stavros's legs and arms up to hoover underneath his unconscious body, sprawled out in the corridor. Not even the thunderous sound of a vacuum cleaner only inches away from his ears could wake him. It was some start to our return to Jersey!

I can barely recall any details whatsoever about the gigs we played out there on that trip, but I can instantly conjure up memories of being in the hotel jacuzzi, and Pablo and Stavros couldn't get out, as they were occupied by a girl's unique massage method, using her feet. Lekiki jumping off the very top of the hotel's intimidating Olympic diving board and not being able to walk for the rest of the day, as he had split his difference (maybe he should have seen old "foot loose and fancy free" for one of her special treatments). Breaking into the reception area to make an announcement over the hotel's PA system for the attention of the Dance Stance party "We have scored some uppers, please meet in reception for consumption!" Instead of giving us a bollocking, the ladies behind the reception desk gave us their phone numbers and their address to pop by later! It was like a *Carry On* film, you couldn't make it up, one barmy and bizarre incident and escapade after another.

I remember there was one moment during the whole of that trip when I really needed to go back to the sanity and solace of my hotel room and have a couple of hours' sleep. I walked in, and there was another girl I hadn't seen before, ironing all of Hammy's clothes for him. When we finally ran out of drugs, we went in search of the local pharmacy to buy up all the packets of *Dodo*, which were like a form of *Pro-plus*, only much stronger; anything to stay wired. We were having the time of our young lives. Sleep could wait.

Thankfully, my dad remained blissfully unaware of our antics after that first day, and I didn't want to cause him any more stress. Emo attended court while we were out there, and took his punishment. The other lad, on a more serious charge of Class A had to fly back out a couple of weeks later to have his hearing. To this day I don't know the extent of their fines, but I'm pretty sure that my dad took care of it all, even organizing and funding the return journey. Nothing more was really said about that aspect of our expedition; I guess it was a small price to pay for the riotous adventure that we had. Needless to say, we never got asked back for a third year by Jersey's tourism board. It would have been less hassle for them to book the Happy Mondays. A friend of mine lives out there now, and he always takes great amusement in telling me that when he's asked where he originally comes from, and answers Atherstone, that more often than not someone will say to him "Do you remember a band called Dance Stance?"

9 – THE BOY HAIRDRESSER

Hairdressing, or more specifically barbering, had been a tradition throughout the years in Hammy's family. His own father, Paul, trained as a barber, and his uncle Larry traded for many years in Atherstone's Market Square, so it was no surprise that Paul Jnr. himself enrolled on a college course after leaving school, and also studied the craft of hair-styling, a profession suited to his modernist and dapper character. After initially getting some hands-on experience at his uncle's shop, Hammy got his first permanent placement just down the road in Market Street, at *Stephen's hairdressers*, which was predominately a ladies' salon. While he was pleased to find gainful employment and some full-time involvement in the trade, washing and drying old ladies' coiffures wasn't exactly what he had in mind. It would be a year or so later, when Hammy returned to his uncle Larry's premises, that he became accustomed to and comfortable with the magical world of the barber shop. Larry was due to retire, and wanted to move the shop on. His daughters had it for a while, and attempted to turn it into a beauty salon, but long-term it was destined to remain a barbershop. Uncle Larry and Hammy came to an agreement, and the lease on the property, which included the flat above the shop, was soon turned over to Hammy. He had his own barbers. He was in business.

Larry, god rest his soul, was a charming gent, and very schooled in the old ways of traditional barbering. I guess he was Hammy's mentor and teacher in many aspects, when it came to learning how to cut hair, but like many of the old traditionalists it is not always to everyone's taste, and really, the likelihood of you getting a decent crop differed from day to day. When he first started working in the barbers, I recall coming home from college one afternoon hoping to catch Hammy to get a little tidy up. This was when he was still working alongside Larry. He wasn't in, but I decided to let Larry do the honours anyway; what is the worst that could happen? Hairdressers, they like to talk, don't they? At the time, I had a full enough head of hair to be sporting a kind of backcombed Stevie Marriott affair; I was still fully modded-up at this point. So, Larry is chatting away to me, snipping, cutting and shearing off my locks. As we converse, I am starting to get a little worried, but foolishly do not intervene. (Stefan in Mancetter was the same, if you got him talking about his tomato plants you could soon enough find yourself with a shorn scalp). He must have detected the look of horror on my face as he placed the mirror at the back of my neck, and proclaimed proudly “There you go Sheas – Cliff Richard!” – Cliff fucking Richard! Keith Richard I could have coped with, but here I am, a fourteen-year-old mod with a DA. I was crestfallen, and of course, on the short walk back to my mum and dad’s, I literally bumped into just about everyone I had ever known from town, all looking curiously at my *Expresso Bongo* quiff. They probably thought Billy Fury had joined The Jam. Oddly enough, a couple of years later; it did actually become my hairstyle of choice for a while.

Hammy was no different. He followed suit, and was equally as unpredictable and erratic with a pair of scissors in his hands as the old guard were. But Hammy had good reason for this; the quality of the haircut you received was really down to what time of day you caught him. Once Hammy took over the shop and got himself established, his barbers became part of town folklore. It was certainly an experience. Don’t get me wrong, Hammy wasn’t work-shy, he just worked to live, the emphasis as always with him being on having the best time possible. That rule applied whether he was out with the band singing, or whether he was cutting hair. Every day was an adventure. Once he made enough money to cover that week’s rent, anything else was a bonus, play money. So, he would take his foot off the gas, just do what he needed to, and the other hours would be spent in search of a good time, usually involving heading off to the pub for the day once the money was made, or taking a friend or two up to the flat to skin up, play some sounds and get slowly stoned. You had to catch him in the morning. He had two signs, one which read *Back in ten mins*, which meant he’s either in the pub or he’s upstairs rolling up, but either way he’s coming back at some point; anything may happen, but you’ll get your hair cut, you’ve just got to cross your fingers, take your chances and hope for the best. The other sign read *Gone to lunch*, which meant he’s either in the pub or he’s upstairs rolling up, but the day’s done, he’s made what little he needs, and the full-on session is in progress, the shop is closed. More often than not, I was usually party to the *Gone to lunch* sessions.

One summer afternoon, when it was far too hot to be doing anything other than sit in a beer garden watching the world go by, there were a few of us in tow (there was usually an entourage to entertain). Certainly, Phil (Ford) was with us, and Hammy made his exit from the barbers as soon as the clock approached a time that was passable to class as lunch. I think the sign went on around 11 a.m. that day, and we pulled on a few spliffs, then made our way into town for refreshments. It was one of those rare but beautiful days when time seems to stand still, and becomes irrelevant. We had ourselves a good walk round the boozers, and were pretty much all well on our way as we turned the corner back up Market Street, heading back to the flat to roll a few more joints. Suddenly, Hammy stops dead in his tracks and tries to scurry back around the corner. But it's too late. He's already been spotted by a queue of at least a dozen people waiting at the door of the barbers, lined along the pavement, waiting to get their hair cut. He's only put the *Back in ten mins* sign up by mistake! It's now 4pm … I think he managed to get through the first two punters and provide them with at least something that kind of resembled what they asked for, before turning everyone else away, kicking them out, asking if they could come back in the morning.

Over the years, it became a regular hangout for friends and waifs and strays alike, and once in a while, they may even get their hair cut. A mate of ours, Tony Coils, decided to be particularly brave one day, and let Hammy bleach his hair for him. Tony was into the Scooter scene in a big way, and he was one of the first of us to sport the rather odd look of having a short crew cut, with a long fringe drooping down to cover the forehead. It became fashionable for a while to get the fringe part-dyed, or bleached a light blonde colour, and so Tony placed this task into Hammy's capable (?) hands. Thankfully, I was there to watch the comedy unfold. The bleach takes a while to set, and the face obviously has to be shielded, especially when it's so close to your eyes. The fringe is covered in tin foil while it takes. So, Tony is kind of oblivious to what is about to happen. Hammy wants to check that everything is in place before he leaves it to settle, and asks Tony to lift his head up a little. As he requests this, he touches the sides of Tony's head, and tilts it upwards slightly. Here's where the fun begins... Hammy has momentarily forgotten that he's still got some bleach on his fingers, and now Tony has two bleached fingerprints about an inch above his ears, either side of his head. Hammy's eyes widen in shock as he realises. He turns to me, trying to suppress his laughter, and signals for me to try and not let on. For reasons known only to himself, Hammy decides that he may as well get arty with the bleach, and square it with Tony once the veils are lifted, and so he proceeds to extend the two little spots where the fingerprints have made an impression into horizontal stripes, like a tiger. Then he gets carried away, and somewhat unbelievably, paints a diamond shape in bleach on top of Tony's head! By this time, we have towels in our mouths to try and stop our howls of laughter. My ribs actually felt like they were turning inside out, I was laughing so much.

"You're going back a bit far there, ain't you, old lad?" enquires Tony from under the covers.
"You've got a high hairline Tone", Hammy reassures him, fighting back tears of laughter.

As Tony Coils is waiting for his new, ultra-hip, scooter-boy bleached fringe to take hold, we can clearly see Hammy's accessorised additions, the striped tramlines and the bold diamond shape, turning a sharp shade of peroxide blonde. Hammy peels off the foil from the fringe (which has also taken to perfection) and then takes the blinkers off Tone to reveal one crazy fucking hair do...

"WHAT THE FUCK!" cries Tony. "ME DADS GONNA FUCKIN' KILL ME!" ...

I must admit, once he calmed down a bit, we did all agree that it did look kind of good, although his dad did indeed go apeshit, and Tone was up pronto the next day to get the diamond and the stripes erased.

I spent many hours drinking endless cups of tea (and beer) in that shop. Hammy never even changed the sign over the front of the shop, and this dated back to the short period I previously mentioned, when Larry's daughters looked after the shop and tried to introduce sunbeds etc. and turn it into a beauty parlour. They named the premises *Mantrap*. So, for a good while, Hammy's barbers had the moniker *Mantrap* outside. I used to love answering the phone, much to the annoyance of Hammy, and greeting callers in the campest of tones "Hello Maantwap, Paul speaking, how may I help Sir?" I would whisper effeminately. Another associate of ours, John Downing, phoned up once to play a trick on Hammy. John knew that Hammy had a heart of gold, and hardly ever said no to people, so he called up and pretended to represent a care worker who had a load of disabled kids that wanted their hair cutting. If he brought them all down in a minibus the next day, could he do it for them?

Phil, Emo and I saw Hammy that night. We were all in on Downing's prank, and Hammy was fretting. "Can I charge them? At least I'll make some good money."

We questioned his morals and looked aghast, winding him up further. "You can't charge them Hammy."
"I wonder how many there's gonna be? A minibus full, he said on the phone ... I mean, how disabled are they gonna be? How I am going to get them to sit still? ... Sheas, can't you come and help me?" I think he was fairly relieved when Downing turned up laughing his bollocks off at the allotted appointment time, rather than a bus full of kids.

He was equally relieved on the occasion when one of the local nutcases came into the shop blind drunk, and demanded to have a skinhead. Hammy did his best to talk him out of it, but the guy insisted on having a number one crop all over, and what made it even more difficult was the fact that Hammy knew that this geezer always kept his fringe long to cover up a tattoo that was engraved on his forehead. He also knew that the guy was really drunk, and that as soon as he sobered up and realised the severity of his new "Skin" look, it would be Hammy himself who would cop the repercussions. In this instance, Hammy boxed clever. He took his time, just trimming the back of the nutter's hair first, hoping that once he settled into the chair he would be so pissed that he would drop off to sleep. Paul Jnr's plan worked to perfection. The guy dozed off in a drunken haze, and woke an hour later, wondering what the fuck he was doing at the barbers, and also, thankfully, with a full head of hair intact, having totally no recollection of wanting to have his head shaved.

People very often speak to me of their memories and recollections of that barbers shop. It's funny to hear their tales and stories, and pretty much everyone that walked through the door has at least one. Only recently, a respectable elderly gentleman shared a recollection of foolishly advising his young son to try Hammy's shop. "I sent our Danny down to see Hammy to get his hair cut when he was about thirteen years old, and he came back with a fucking ganja leaf shaved into the back of his hair!" I do actually know folk who still sport scars around their ears from where he had slipped with his scissors. Youths would have nicks, cuts and snips all around their neck, but they'd go back time and time again just for the experience and the banter with him. Most punters would usually end up visiting Dave down at Stefan's in Mancetter, and paying again just to get Hammy's efforts finished off properly. But you can dare bet that they were back again in Hammy's chair next time they were in need of a trim, just for the entertainment. In fact, I even knew several women that went to him. It was only hair after all.

1986, sunglasses indoors

Atherstone Town FC, **Sheepy Road, October 1971, aged four**

With Mum and Dad, Croyde Bay, July 1970

Musical youth, makeshift drum kit

Me and Nick Thomas, Blackpool, 1975

Majorca, 1984, Hammy, my dad and me

Carnaby Street, early 80s, Hammy and I

The In Crowd, *Atherstone Football Club*, 1983

Early Dance Stance line up, 1985 with the Delaney brothers

Spain, 1985

Early 80s, with Nicolette, Ita and Paul Hanlon snr.

Dance Stance, 1987 (Photo, Steve Ellis)

Left to right:
Andy Codling, Guy Greenway, Paul Tunicliffe, Dave Delaney, Hammy, Nick Read, Phil Ford, Dik Delaney and myself.
Shackerstone Train Station

With Nick Read, London, 1989

Italy, 1988

Cloisters Wine Bar, Long Street, Atherstone – with Edwin Starr

Grappling with credibility and conscience, *BBC Op Knocks* with Bob Monkhouse

TV / *BBC* Dance Stance

Me, Nick Read and Hammy with Ron and Melisa Goodyear, Orton on the Hill, 1989

Rare Future

Boys to men, with Jasmine (above) and Mason (below)

Paul Hanlon (AKA, Hammy)

Hammy, Tiffany's, Coventry aged 13 (Photo: Toni Tye)

Myself and Claire, 1996 and 2019

10 - MAGIC AND LOSS

"Excuse me mate, you don't know what these auditions are for by any chance, do you?" enquired Coddy. Somehow, we find ourselves at the *BBC* Television studios in Nottingham, preparing to audition for what we had been reliably informed is a new TV music programme. So, naturally, we presume that we are about to get a chance at appearing on the first series of a cutting-edge live music show that will be the *BBC's* answer to *The Tube*, which has proven to be a great success for *Channel 4*. As we are ushered to a changing room, it resembles more like a scene from *Billy Smart's Circus* than *The Old Grey Whistle Test*; there's jugglers in corridors, young kids limbering up in dance troupes, and, like the figure standing in front of us dealing with Coddy's question, old blokes in full dinner suit and cabaret attire. Something doesn't add up.

Mr. Entertainment looks at us down his nose in utter disgust, as he slips on his spats.

"*Op Knocks*", he replies.

"*Op Knocks*?" I intervene. "Not *Opportunity* fucking *Knocks*?"

Our hearts collectively drop. Coddy, usually the most reserved of all of us, is incensed with rage, and is ready to depart the building immediately. I think it was Pablo who played the diplomat, and convinced us that having made the journey, we may as well stay, and go through with the charade, if only for comedy value. After all, a prime time Saturday night TV show is not going to be remotely interested in a bunch of tearaways like us, peddling our own brand of rock 'n' soul music, and to be honest, neither would we expect or want them to be. So, after a few moans and groans aimed in my dad's direction, we reluctantly agreed to stay and experience the faintly bizarre spectacle and farce of the initial rounds of *Opportunity Knocks* auditions. I think dad must have known what he was getting us involved in, but probably never realised what resistance and outrage he would encounter from us.

The first thing you instantly pick up on is how desperate people are to get on TV; even the young kids take themselves far too seriously. It was like a hundred and one Working Men's club and cabaret acts all gathered for that one elusive crack at stardom, longing for their fifteen minutes of fame, a scene both hilarious and pitiful in equal measures. We looked on, fascinated by the parade of hopefuls, from operatic Maria Callas wannabes, to a bunch of old sweats covering Cockney Rebel, all pursuing their dream of being discovered via TV's top talent show. For our part, I think we selected the most unsuitable song of ours we could think of, and gave a complete non-performance, with a total disdain and disinterest for our surroundings and the absurdity of the audition process. We got it over and done with, found the nearest pub, and enjoyed the rest of our day. My dad made some half-hearted attempt to justify why he had attempted to put us up for a slot on the nation's favourite light-entertainment show in front of fifteen million viewers, but quickly realised that it was never going to happen, and our brief foray into the world of showbiz was quickly forgotten about.

Towards the back end of that summer of 1988, just a month or two short of my twenty-first birthday, my dad had been signed off work, and ordered to rest up for a while. This in itself was something of a shock to us, as he never got ill. I can't even recall him having a cold, and a trip to the doctor's was virtually unheard of. But he'd been complaining of chest pains, and was getting breathless, so he decided to get himself checked out. It was diagnosed as angina, which can of course, in some cases, be a serious indicator of an impending heart attack. It certainly slowed him down somewhat, and he appeared drained and tired, so we decided to take a family holiday to Italy, just me, my dad, my mum and Rachel, my girlfriend at the time, in an attempt to help him relax and recuperate. The change of pace and climate seemed to work wonders, and we spent an unhurried, peaceful week together. My dad seemed at ease and untroubled, and it was great to have the time to dig in, to talk and reflect with him. I felt like we were entering another stage of our father and son bond, as adults, and it was one I was looking forward to. I returned from that break contented and carefree, confident that my dad was on the mend, and that our anxieties concerning his health and well-being could be soon put to rest. I fell in love with Italy in those few days too. The lifestyle is leisurely, almost at walking pace compared with the stress and strife of the UK, the food was magnificent everywhere we went, and of course the Italians always keep a sharp eye on their clothes. I came back with an extra suitcase full of shirts.

I had a landmark birthday on the horizon that October, which we celebrated by doing a gig at the *Polytechnic* in Stoke on the Friday night. It is memorable for the fact that we all experimented with some tiny capsules that were pushed in our direction, and sold to us as the closest thing that was currently on the market to a *Dexedrine* bomber, the speed rush of choice for original Mods of the 1960s. How could we resist? The gig was an adrenaline-fuelled, highly charged celebratory affair, and one of our best. When we all reconvened at my mum and dad's house on the Sunday, which was the 16th, and the day of my actual twenty-first birthday, all of us had eyeballs as wide as saucers, hadn't slept or eaten since the Friday, and looked like we were wired to the moon, still buzzing from the rush of the tablets.

"You eaten yet?", "You slept yet?" were the immediate topics of conversation as we greeted each other, all of us still nervously twitching, and chewing furiously on our own gums.

Nick Read had called me a few hours before the gathering, asking if he could bring a date with him, a new girlfriend he had taken out a couple of times. I was so paranoid from the whizz that I wouldn't let her in the house at first, as I was convinced she was a strip-o-gram. "Fuck off, you ain't coming in. I'm not into being embarrassed and having my clothes stripped off. You can fuck off, I know what you're up to", were my first words to Nick's new girlfriend Sonia, who he went out with for several more years. I don't think she ever really warmed to me.

We had a good day of it, fired the sound system up, and had a Sunday all-dayer to mark my coming of age. My mum made some food that we all just stared at, wondering if we would ever regain something that resembled an appetite. My dad remained fairly quiet throughout the day, the lads in the band taking it in turns to pop their heads into the living room and have a natter with him, and he seemed in good spirits. It was several days before normal service was fully resumed. Those tiny capsules were like rocket fuel. You certainly wouldn't put on much timber on a staple diet of those things. Hammy discovered another couple of them in his jacket pocket as me and him travelled to a Martin Stephenson and The Daintees gig at *Loughborough University* a few days later. We had only just about regained some sort of routine and stability after swallowing the last lot, so we decided to pass on another ride in the fast lane, although little did I know at this point that I was about to miss out on a lot more sleep over the forthcoming weeks. But in very different circumstances.

We didn't make it straight home after the Daintees gig, taking a detour over to Nuneaton, where our shop, *What Records*, was hosting a party until the early hours at *Rumours* nightclub. I can't even recall what the occasion was, but I do remember there were a couple of bands on, and it was an excuse for a late drink before heading home. It must have been around 3am when I got back and headed straight for bed. I awoke a few hours later, and got myself ready for another day at the shop in Bedworth. I didn't see my dad that morning; he was still in bed, which was unusual for him, as he was always up and about first thing, even while on leave from work.

It was business as usual at the shop. I felt slightly tired from my late night escapades, but it was nothing unusual for me to be burning the candle at both ends back then, as twenty-one year-olds do. A few local DJs had started to filter in early, and I was busy playing and selling them the latest releases when the phone rang. Cheryl, the girl who worked with me at the time, answered it. Something wasn't right. She looked at me as she put down the receiver with a grief stricken, ashen face. The colour had drained from her appearance. "You need to go home Neil, your dad has taken a turn for worse", she said.

"A turn for the worse?" I repeated, "What does that mean?"

I knew, of course. I felt it. That car ride back from Bedworth to Atherstone seemed to take forever. I played out various scenarios in my head; maybe he had just had a fall? Or didn't feel too good again and was having to go into hospital? "A turn for the worse". I knew exactly what that meant. Tears ran down my cheeks as I tried my hardest to brace myself for the worst possible scenario. Of course, it doesn't matter how hard you try, nothing can prepare you for experiencing death for the first time. Or at any time for that matter, especially immediate family, particularly your father. That bond is irreplaceable.

Finally, after that dreamlike journey, feeling like I was driving in slow motion, I returned home to find my mum in floods of tears, unable to speak, paralysed by shock and grief, and being comforted by a neighbour. I dash up to the bedroom, where my dad lies motionless on the bed, quiet and still. I lie down beside him and hug him for the last time, knowing that I am completely helpless to change this situation. I can almost feel my heart breaking in two. A very surreal feeling sweeps through me as though this isn't really happening to us, that he will wake up and speak to me as if he has just been in a deep sleep. But tragically this is very real, and Dad won't be waking next to me, not now, not ever again. He is gone. Momentarily, the world felt as if it had stopped spinning. I was in freeze-frame. Shocked and confused, it was like a thunderbolt had hit me, and I was numb with fear. My dad was dead.

The days and weeks that followed were pretty much a daze. You can't really adjust to such a sudden loss. To all intents and purposes, I probably appeared to be coping quite well with it at the time, and remained strong for my mum, to get her through it all, but inside I was mortified, crippled by sadness and an overwhelming sense of emptiness. But what else can you do, but just face up to the reality of the situation, and simply get on with trying to reassemble the pieces of your life? It felt like a momentous task, but I couldn't let myself drown in sorrow at twenty-one years old. I had to pull myself together and get on with life.

The funeral was a complete blur. A sea of faces gathered to pay their respects, work colleagues, old football acquaintances, family, lifelong friends. I'm sure most of them spoke to me to offer their thoughtful, kind words of condolence, but I didn't really hear them. I wasn't even able to properly see the gathered mass of gracious well-wishers in attendance that day. It was all a fog. The vicar spoke, but it wasn't really Dad he spoke about. It could have been anyone's life he was summarizing and paying respect to, and once again, I felt totally numb, removed from it all, as if I was in a film, and how I wished that the director would call 'cut' and we would return to normality. I didn't even cry; I wasn't able to. I think I wanted to experience that release, but it never came. I was still so locked up in shock. I do recall that the only time when my emotions came flooding out was down at the cemetery, as his coffin was lowered into the ground, and the earth was scattered onto it. That seemed final. A symbolic ritual that signalled our final goodbye. I was devastated.

The lads in the band had carried his coffin in and out of the church, and they remained solid at my side throughout. I tried to get pissed with them later that day, but however much I drank, it had absolutely no effect upon me. This sorrow would not be drowned. It would take time, more than a few lost weekends, and an enormous strength of character to pull through. Fittingly enough, music was my comfort blanket once again on that night of his funeral. After everyone else had departed, and my mum had emotionally exhausted herself and gone off to bed, I fired up the stereo and played Talk Talk's *Spirit Of Eden* album on a constant loop until daylight appeared. That particular sprawling masterpiece had only just been released back then in the September of 1988. I was almost instantly floored by its sheer beauty, and it has remained a record that I have consistently returned to for moments of solace and reflection. I don't think I have ever listened to it with anyone else in the room. It demands your attention. You couldn't possibly have a conversation during it. I think it is a timeless piece of work, and if I heard it for the first time tomorrow, it would sound as relevant, and as fresh and as challenging as it did back then. It would almost definitely qualify for my *Desert Island Disc*. That night it provided me with a glimmer of reassurance and hope that the world would seem a brighter place again sometime soon, even if, right then, the cruel hand of fate hid the rainbow.

The few months that followed were hard to cope with. The huge shift in personal circumstance was really hard to adjust to. I thought he would come walking through the door again at any point, and we would just get on with life, as we'd always known it. I kind of kept it all bottled up inside me, as I wanted to remain strong and be supportive for my mum, whose own world had been turned upside down so dramatically. They had been together since she was a young teenager. Dad had been at her side for forty years. As much as I intended to be a rock and a pillar of stability for her, I went off the fucking rails. Only Hammy and my other bandmates kept me from pending disaster. The overriding emotion I felt at the time was anger, but I also felt some self-pity. "Why me?" I constantly thought. My emotions were numbed for a while. I had been hurt so much that I think I felt nothing else could possibly damage me. I'd take out my frustration on others, sometimes looking for an argument, or to start a fight just to vent my inner anguish, pain and torment. I was in a mess.

As always, my medicine and my comfort would be found through channelling all my energies into creating music. In the initial aftermath of my father's death though, even the band had pretty much ground to a standstill. As much as the lads rallied around me to keep me in check, I think they themselves were deeply saddened and shocked by his passing. Fortunately for all of us, our saviour was about to reveal himself, and kick-start our musical escapades back into full throttle.

I first met Al Calnan when he was managing a group called 'Written In Yellow', who also hailed from the Midlands. We had played a couple of university gigs alongside them, and Al was always both very friendly towards us and complimentary about our music. He hit it off with my dad right from the start, and in hindsight, I think Dad had found someone in Al that he could trust to eventually step into his shoes and manage the band, meaning he didn't constantly have to be on the road with us. I am certain that is what was on my dad's mind, but he just never got the opportunity to put the proposal to Al. As it turned out, one of the first band-related calls I received after my dad's death was from Al, saying that we had to continue, that he would be willing to take over the reins for a while, and that he would help us find our feet and get the band out gigging and recording again. Eventually, after a month or so, I did feel the urge to get out and play a few gigs again. There's no better cure for mourning than getting back among friends. It's heartening just how supportive people can be when it's obvious that you are grieving and in need of a lift. It's an old worn out cliché, but time is a healer, and as the man once said ... all things must pass.

Our first venture back into the fray was intended to be a low-key affair, a charity event, held in the miniscule confines of our local wine bar on Long Street. Normally I wouldn't have even entertained the idea of cramming an eight-piece line-up into the corner of a room that actually struggled to house no more than a handful once the band has set up, but it had been a regular haunt of ours for quite some time, and the owners had been good to us. It was a real music place too. For a while, it was run by a gay guy who called himself Yan, although his real name was Mick. His taste in music was impeccable, and I think it was he who first turned us on to the delights of Betty Wright and William De Vaughn. I certainly liked hanging out there; it was a culture bunker, you would always learn something, and the food was incredible while Mick/Yan was running the show.

This particular night, the night we decided to shake the walls of the wine bar, was in recognition of what had been raised from a previous event. A cheque was to be presented to the benefactors, the local press were invited to cover proceedings, and we had agreed to perform on the night for no other reason than to dust off any cobwebs, and get us, especially me, out playing music again. What we didn't know until we turned up on the night, was that they had invited a local celebrity along to present the cheque. This was none other than US *Tamla Motown* soul-singing sensation Edwin Starr, who had now been residing in the stately grounds of *Pooley Hall* in nearby Polesworth for the last few years. Nobody was quite sure if Edwin was actually going to turn up or not, and when he did duly show up, I'm certain it was with the intention of handing over the cheque, smiling for a couple of pictures for the benefit of the local papers, and then shooting straight back off again. That was until he noticed a band was set up. And not just any band … these cats carried a horn section. Edwin was intrigued, and stuck around to see what was in store.

We were busy getting tanked up on cans of *Budweiser* in the kitchen when word reached us that Edwin Starr was in the building, and that he'd made himself comfortable to catch our gig. It had only been a few years previously that myself and Hammy had witnessed Edwin and his band thrill the masses gathered at *Hinckley Leisure Centre*, at one of their notorious northern soul all-nighters. So we had the utmost respect for him, and wanted to be on top of our game. I mean, it's not every day a bona fide soul legend is sitting in a minute wine bar in the middle of Atherstone waiting to watch you play.

It wasn't long before Edwin was out of his seat, and had his eyes and ears firmly fixed upon us. We had caught his attention alright! I sensed what was coming, and after we had played a soul-stomping hour's set, he was itching to get up and sing with us. Of course, this was absolutely fine by us. As we took a break, Edwin approached us, introduced himself, and asked us if we knew anything that he might know. As luck had it, we had only just dumped a cover from our live set of *(I can't get no) Satisfaction*, which merged straight into a version of *Respect*, both usually played at breakneck speed, complete with relentless, driving horn riffs. By now, word had spread around the pubs in town that Edwin Starr was in the wine bar, and was probably going to get up and do a turn with Dance Stance.

The place was absolutely heaving by the time Edwin and Hammy squared up to sing together. Folk were stood on chairs and tables, faces were pressed against every outside window, and sweat was dripping off the ceiling. Phil clicked the sticks, and we fired into gear. Hammy, who was no slouch as a singer, set the pace … *I can't get no satisfaction, no I can't get no satisfaction ... cause I try... and I try ... I try ... but I can't get no ...*

What happened next will stay with me to my dying day. In recent times I've been fortunate enough to work and play bass for some of the most wonderful and unique singers in Black American soul music, really great singers of that generation such as Joe "Pep" Harris and Nolan Porter, but I can honestly say I have never heard a voice as colossal as Edwin Starr's, which was even more exaggerated in the small surroundings of Atherstone's wine bar. On this particular night, you could physically hear the first notes that came from his mouth swelling up from his stomach and just erupt around the room *....wwwwwwWWW...WHEN I'M DRIVIN' IN MY CAR AND THAT MAN COMES ON THE RADIO ...*

I remember looking across at Hammy, and his face was a picture. He just started cracking up with laughter. Nick Read and I caught each other's glances, and we both had tears welling up in our eyes. I think the brass section almost shit themselves, and Phil just started pounding the drums harder and harder. What a fucking spectacle it must have been to witness! The whole room just caught fire, one of those rare and magical moments, and unrepeatable.

Edwin was the first bona fide soul star we ever got to play with. It was a shock to hear such a powerful voice in a man, but it was so controlled, and his phrasing just kept throwing up surprise after surprise as he worked his way around the songs. It was truly exciting, and I think for him too, as to be fair, he was used to his comfort zone, and his pick-up bands that I had seen him play with in those times were a bit lame and cabaret, like most covers bands or function bands usually are. They just get lazy, and are there for the cheque at the end of the night, instead of putting in the extra yard and creating something of far greater worth. Edwin sensed this connection immediately. He knew instantly that we were the perfect band for him, and I'm sure we could have spent the next few years earning a few quid as Edwin's band, but as much as that would have been enjoyable, we had our own thing to do. We were about today, the here and now, not a nostalgic soul revue. I know he and his manager (who was his German wife), persisted in trying to hijack our brass section for a while after that night.

Another of my other overriding memories from that night was Edwin lecturing us on the perils of drink and drugs. He would keep repeating the phrase "Drink? Drugs? That's a No-No!" Of course, we often called upon this mantra over the next few months when we found ourselves pissed out of our faces or stoned out of our minds. He wouldn't even be photographed with us if we had a can of beer in our hand. At that time in our young hedonistic lives, it would have never worked out between us and Edwin.

Al Calnan, the man responsible for trying to get us back out on the road again, was also there to witness that night, and it was the validation and confirmation that he needed to place his belief in us. He was quick to tell me that it was remarkable how we just got something together in an instant to play with Edwin, and weren't at all overawed by the situation. In fact, we rose to it, and made it one for the memory banks. He told me that the other bands he managed would have just crumbled on the spot. He was right, and it was just the tonic and lift that I needed after a dark and disastrous few months to end 1988.

11- TRIPPING OVER OPPORTUNITY (88 INTO 89)

With the stress and the trauma catching up with me, I was feeling completely out of sorts by the end of the year, and I'd almost convinced myself that I would keel over at any point and have a heart attack of my own. Reluctantly, I forced myself to go to the doctor's, a place I thankfully seldom visit. He called it anxiety, and prescribed me capsules called *beta-blockers*, which just made me feel like I was constantly stoned, and slowed me down to the point where I could barely string two sentences together. I lasted about one week in a comatose zombie-like trance before Hammy suggested that I should either bin them or sell them. They certainly made me feel about ten times worse; I could barely function, and fuck knows how I used to drive my car to the record shop! I remember getting there and just sitting on top of the gas heater all day, staring into space, having the occasional jolt of reality, and wondering how on earth I'd even driven myself the twenty or so miles that I had to travel every day. I dumped the tablets, and worked my own way through it all, gradually reassembling some sort of normality in my life.

The first real major hurdle in the aftermath of Dad's death was Christmas. Traditionally a time for families, I knew it was going to be a testing and tough time for both me and mum. Looking back, I think we were both still a bit shell-shocked and fairly numb, but we muddled on through, and adjusted to our (now very different) lives the best we possibly could. I pretty much stayed rooted at home, trying to make sure mum was OK, but my overbearing concerns were getting to the point where I was hardly going out myself, and in the end mum virtually booted me out the door, so I could see my mates and just get on with living, and doing the things a twenty-one-year-old should be doing over Christmas. On the evening of Christmas Day itself, Hammy decided to have a party at the flat that he shared with Delisha, his girlfriend at the time, in the Market Square. It was the ideal opportunity for me to get out of the house, indulge myself in some Christmas spirit, and forget about any sorrow and strife that I was feeling. However, I wasn't quite prepared for the indulgence and escapism that was to follow. Hammy was determined to brighten up my mood and give me a much-needed lift. Just being around him naturally made me momentarily forget any woe or worry, but he was quite adamant that we should have ourselves the best time possible, and of course as always, Hammy had an idea.

Our mate Emo (the minder of our cannabis on the ill-fated Jersey trip) was in attendance at the gathering, and I was summoned in a kind of secretive fashion into the kitchen for a briefing. Emo and Hammy had a plan. Emo had got his hands on some acid tabs with the dubious moniker of "Nut Nut", and quite fancied the experience of tripping the light fantastic. Not wanting to be wired to the moon alone, he had decided that a better idea would be to rope me and Hammy in, and all have the trip together. Hammy agreed that this was perfect, but I begged to differ. In the not-too-distant past, I had already been hoodwinked into getting stoned in the afternoons, and necking speed capsules that had kept me awake without food for a week. I liked a good drink, but always pretty much kept my feet on the floor. I had no great curiosity or desire to partake in a re-enactment of *Woodstock*, or float off to a destination unknown. As always my colleagues, in particular Hammy, were quite persuasive in convincing me that I'd be missing out on the time of my life, and how wonderful and hilarious this daring adventure would be. In my naivety, I honestly had no idea what to expect. What was the worst that could happen? I was in need of a lift anyway; I just hadn't quite anticipated how high. I washed down the tiny microdot object that was in my hand with a swig of beer, and awaited my fate. I had arrived at the party with my girlfriend at the time, Rachael. I decided she need not know of my chemical indulgence, and if my behaviour became erratically suspicious I would just blame it on the buffet; there being far too many pickled onions …

An hour or so must have passed, and I'd felt zero effect. My feet were still firmly planted on the ground. Towards midnight, I decided to call it a night. As this was the first Christmas that my mum had spent home alone in the aftermath of my father's death, I thought it only right to head home early. News of my premature departure from the party rang alarm bells with Hammy and Emo - "No way man! You can't go now! Your high is about to kick in. You can't go? We have to stay together". I explained that I hadn't felt anything, I was fine, and obviously my system was immune to acid trips! Off I set on the short walk back down to my mum's house on Friary Road. No sooner had I taken my shoes off than I became intensely engrossed in what she was watching on the television, a late-night screening of a benefit gig to save the rain forests. Sting was making an impassioned speech, before introducing Youssou

N'Dour and his band on stage. Without really noticing, I found myself completely engrossed in the TV; actually, to be more precise, I'd lost the context of the TV screen, and placed myself on stage with Youssou and his band … I pitched my congas stage left, on the end of the row of African musicians, and began to play. First requirement was to take my shirt off - it was sure to be a hot gig - then I quickly found my rhythm, and set about getting absolutely immersed in my debut gig on congas and percussion with Youssou N'Dour.

It wasn't until my mum broke the spell by asking what the hell I was doing that I suddenly had a jolt of reality, and realised that I wasn't actually on stage with Youssou N'Dour at all, but was instead tripping my fucking tits off on "Nut Nut" acid, and was stood to the side of my mum's telly with my top off, sweating my bollocks off, playing an imaginary set of congas.

"What's up with you? What you been drinking?" my mum enquired.

"Oh, nothing mum, I just think I overdid it on the buffet; too many pickled onions I reckon, mum ..." I thought it best to attempt to sit down for a moment and do my best to straighten myself out. Youssou's set had ended anyway now, and given way to an appeal by Peter Gabriel. Peter Gabriel doesn't smile much. He's quite an intense, serious kind of character at the best of times, so when he's spouting out the ramifications of global warming and the implications of losing half of the Amazon's rain forests, then it ain't exactly comedy gold, and I can assure you that if you've recently swallowed a tab of acid, then Peter Gabriel on a downer is the last fucking face you want to be confronted with on your television screen. I can't even look at him to this day for fear of a flashback; freaked me out proper! I thought in that moment that the end of the world was pending.

It was time for bed. I was conscious enough of my erratic behaviour to realise that my pickled onion alibi wouldn't keep my already-suspicious mother at bay for much longer, so I made my way upstairs to the safe, solitary haven of my bedroom. Bad move. There was nowhere to hide from this psychedelic onslaught. First up, the red digital numbers on the alarm clock started to freak me out. Their pulsating, illuminating presence filled up the room. I thought they were trying to communicate with me, like *Morse code*. They began to terrify me. Eventually I switched my thoughts on enough to realise I could unplug the clock. Wow, peace at last ... next up, I decide I'm cold. Within moments of arriving at that conclusion, I declare myself freezing! The bedroom may well have turned into a giant refrigerator! It was time to act ... I jumped up out of bed and proceeded to raid my wardrobe in an attempt to find any item of clothing that could keep me from dying of hypothermia. I put on at least four layers, and then I managed to dig out my old parka to wrap around me. I topped my insulation off with a woollen hat, which I found at the back of a bottom drawer. It mattered not that it was an old Leeds United pom-pom hat from the 1970's that I had nostalgically squirrelled away as a childhood keepsake. At this moment in time, it was keeping the heat in. Even with this ludicrous drape of clothing, I convince myself I am still cold. I have to take matters into my own hands and leave the sanctuary of my bedroom to venture down the hall and wake my mother up. I burst into her bedroom layered up with clothing, an old army parka that I haven't worn since school, and a seven-year-old's hat on. I demand for the heating to be switched on immediately; I'm perishing, frozen to my core. My mum just orders me to go back to bed - "What's up with you? You've not been yourself since you came home." I mutter something about pickled onions and retreat back to my bedroom.

Now, after what to me seemed like hours, but in reality was probably about five minutes on from my deep-freeze incident, my frazzled mind, flying ferociously high, decides that I am now boiling hot, roasting ... in fact I can barely breathe with this stifling temperature ... I have to head back down the hallway and alert my mum once more to turn off the heating (which she never put on in the first place) and open some windows ... I'm about to bake in the humidity of the house. But first I have to free myself of clothing. My poor old mother! No doubt still in mourning for her late husband, she is now about to be traumatised by the sight of her only son, bursting into her bedroom completely stark-bollock naked, screaming at her to turn the heating off. As soon as I barked my demands, I had a sudden jolt of reality. I was naked as the day I was born, twenty-one years old, Christmas Day evening, acting like a complete and utter loon in front of my recently widowed mum. Shit. I quickly scurried back to my room, and made sure I stayed there until daylight.

Once I'd fought off the illusion that I was going to swallow my tongue, as it was as heavy as lead, and I'd toyed with the idea of calling the police to tell them my mates were in danger, that they'd taken some hallucinogenic acid tab called "Nut Nut" and they know not what they've done to themselves (talked myself out of that one thankfully), I eventually began to return to a condition that I can remotely describe as normal. I can recall the relief. I turned on the TV at about 6am, as television was yet to continue twenty-four hours through the night in the late 1980's. Programmes were just about to commence on that Boxing Day morning, and the first thing that grabbed my attention was the children's film *Bambi.* I could honestly feel the weight of the previous night's ordeal lift from my shoulders. *Bambi* comforted me and brought me gently back down to earth. By the time I gained enough of a grasp of reality, and some small shred of whatever dignity I had left, I eventually became confident enough to go downstairs. Thankfully some distant relatives were visiting, so I took the opportunity to exchange pleasantries, make my excuses, and nip straight out the front door. It was never mentioned again, nor did I eat pickled onions in my mum's presence after that, just in case it jogged her memory banks. I wouldn't have wanted her to have her own flashbacks now, would I?

As a band, we had settled back into rehearsals in preparation for another tour of the UK's university and college halls, the first date of which was a support slot to the ska group Bad Manners at *Leicester Polytechnic.* We were still allowed to rehearse on the stage of the high school's main hall in Atherstone. This was long after we had finished our educational stint there. I think my old man had come to some arrangement with Stan, the school's caretaker. Everyone had their price, and I don't think it took much of a king's ransom to get Stan to open up on a Sunday afternoon every week, for us to make a racket in the main hall. A day or two before our jaunt was about to commence, and we were in the midst of rehearsing for the Bad Manners gig, Stan came rushing into the hall to interrupt our practice. My mum had phoned saying there was an urgent call awaiting me, and could I nip back home, as it sounded very important and it regarded the band. I needed to return their call as soon as possible. I broke off the rehearsal, and made my way back home, contemplating whether it would be *EMI*, *Virgin* or *Island Records* on the blower, wanting to make negotiations with me after being bowled over by our latest demo.

"Neil, it sounds very exciting", said my mother upon my return. "A lady from the *BBC* rang asking for someone connected to Dance Stance. Sounded important and quite urgent. She's left her number, and wants you to call her back straight away". My heart sank. I knew it could be only one thing, which wasn't news at all. Obviously the *Opportunity Knock*s crew were just doing their courtesy calls to notify all the acts from the final auditions that they hadn't been successful. (I could never for one moment consider us as an 'act'!) Any further thoughts or consideration of preposterous prime time TV slots had long been forgotten, especially after turning up to audition number two half-cut, and Hammy giving the stuffy old producer high fives and soul shakes at every given opportunity. I should point out here that after being completely dismissive of the whole debacle at the first audition and thinking that would be the last we would hear of it, we did actually get invited back for a second audition down at *Riverside Studios* in London. We politely turned down the invitation but the *BBC* insisted and paid for all our travel costs, so we decided we would treat it as a jolly boys outing, a freebie on the *Beeb*. We took the train down, got completely wankered, had a great time around the city, almost forgetting about the auditions, that was just a mere sideshow. Once again we just believed that they had beckoned us down just to confirm that we would be totally unsuitable for their light entertainment parade.

Anyway, I dialled the number scrawled in front of me and made my introduction. The lady on the other end of the line sounded ecstatic, certainly far too cheery for the task of informing hopeful magicians, comedians and crooners that their dreams of TV stardom are shattered.

"I hope you're sitting down", began the fervent, joyful voice on the other end of the line. "I have some amazing news", she enthused, much to my confusion. "Your band is going to be live on the *BBC's* biggest Saturday night TV show! Congratulations, you passed our auditions, and you will be appearing on the next live series of *Bob Says Opportunity Knocks'!* ... Now, if my heart hadn't already sunk low enough to find that it wasn't Richard Branson belling me to offer us a lucrative recording contract, I can tell you my ticker was lurking around my ankles by this point. I was stunned into silence, but unfortunately, for Mrs Buoyant of the *Beeb* on the other end of the phone, it wasn't because I was beside myself with glee. I was fucking mortified. It wasn't long before my disappointed tones registered, and I had to explain myself. Obviously, the *BBC* and their employees were not used to having their offers of television stardom rejected, but here I was about to burst that balloon. I had absolutely no intention of accepting their offer, so did my best to let them down gently, and as politely as I could.

"Oh, that's such a shame, Mr Sheasby, you would have been the highest-paid act we have ever had on the show too ... at least we'll save some money, I suppose"."Woah! What's that?" I quickly replied.

"Well, we pay our featured artists for the five days that they are required, from the Monday to the Friday, and obviously we would be putting you up in a top hotel in Knightsbridge. A coach would pick you up from Atherstone, and then return you home after filming the show on the Friday, ahead of the broadcast on TV Saturday night ... and I believe there are nine of you in the band?"

"Correct… er … yeah".

"And of course I take it that you are all members of the musicians union?"

"Er… oh, yeah, of course!" I cautiously answered. "Well, that would have amounted to some expenditure on the *BBC's* behalf over the five days we would need you for. I can't recall the show paying out so much in expenses on another artist". I took a large gulp, and quickly swallowed my pride, and probably my credibility, before retorting "Can I phone you back in five minutes ...?"

12 - BOB N' BEEB

I realise it sounds slightly mournful, but I actually take some solace and peace of mind from visiting the cemetery. Still to this day, I will regularly drop by if I am in need of a pick-me-up or some inspiration. I always feel a little bit clearer on what path to take, or maybe about a pending decision. Don't get me wrong, I'm not one of those sorts that talks out loud to headstones or anything, I just find it a good place to reflect and think upon life; maybe the surroundings offer a clearer perspective? Whatever my reasons anyway, I find it calming and peaceful. The very morning we were due to be picked up by the *BBC* in a 52-seater luxury coach (for just nine of us), I was restless. I was still mulling over the fact that I had relented, against what was probably my better judgement, and agreed to spend a week in showbiz. The decision pained me, and was still troubling me as I wandered through the gates of Atherstone cemetery as the sun was breaking through the clouds at 7am. Our transport would be waiting for us down at the football club car park in a couple of hours, and I needed to know I had done the right thing. I went and sat by my dad's newly laid headstone for an hour, and gathered my thoughts. After all, he had steered us into this surreal situation.

I was trying to convince myself that by playing the game and gaining prime time exposure on national TV on a Saturday night, we would finally break the band into the public's hearts and minds. Anyone with half a brain would realise that we didn't fit with the other opportunists knocking at the *BBC's* door, the magic acts, or child opera singers or clubland comedians. No, we were the real deal, fish out of water. Surely that would be apparent? I knew it wouldn't quite be a match for the Sex Pistols with Bill Grundy, but Dance Stance on *BBC1* introduced by Bob Monkhouse? I certainly had zero respect for that situation. *The X-Factor* of its time watched by millions, but incredibly naff and trite, I calmed my anxieties by believing that we could hi-jack *Opportunity Knocks* to create our own little stir, and attract some credible attention. I think some of the lads just wanted to be on TV, but that side of things never appealed to me. It still doesn't, but who was I to deny them their five minutes of infamy? Oddly enough at the time, nobody we knew actually thought it was naff, and they all thought we'd hit the jackpot and made it. I was probably alone in my mild embarrassment, and was my own worst enemy and critic. I wrestled with my misgivings and apprehension about relenting, agreeing to appear on what I considered to be a light entertainment façade.

My frustrations were soon cushioned once our weeklong adventure began. After being ferried down to London in style, we soon arrived at the world-famous Broadcasting House in Shepherd's Bush. I had seen that entrance hundreds of times both in newspapers and on TV, so to be ushered through those gates and into the magical inner sanctum of the *BBC* was undeniably thrilling, although it did turn out to be slightly underwhelming. I guess taking a peek behind the *BBC* curtain undid the mystery and intrigue; it was like a glorified technical college complete with shit canteen. We'd only been there about ten minutes, and had already received the frown of scorn from the *Beeb's* high priestess Esther Rantzen, who seemed to be constantly stalking the corridors of power peering down her nose at everyone. I couldn't have given a fuck who she was. We weren't back at school, and even if she played the part of headmistress very well, she had no chance of intimidating us.

The show's production team summoned us to a brief, where they had a set agenda, and a plan to occupy the five days. Most of it didn't really apply to us, for example, wardrobe and styling - we went mainly because Hammy and I wanted to have a nose around the *BBC* costume department. We, of course, had our own look at the time (as always); around this period, we were sporting high-waisted, pleated-front trousers, collarless grandad style shirts, brogues, and demob-style jackets. It was kind of a neater JoBoxers image. I think Brian De Palma's film *The Untouchables* had just been released, and we were certainly influenced by that style-wise, an Italian/New York crossover, done with our unique British tip; always a winner, I suppose. Anyway, if I recall correctly, some of the brass lads managed to blag waistcoats and a few pairs of trousers. Choreography was another day on the production team's agenda. We sent the brass lads in again to represent us, while we retreated to the pub. I kind of regret that, as the instructor turned out to be a bit of a beauty queen, who was certainly more invigorated to be greeted by twenty-one-year-old sprightly youths in a band than some bunch of old sweats plucked directly from the Working Men's clubs of Great Britain. There was one really great moment to emerge from the week's agenda. On the night the show was to be filmed, the vocal would be live, but the rest of the band had to mime to a backing track. At first that seemed like a cop out; I wanted us to play live, as it was what the band prided itself upon, and also how we'd earned our solid reputation from years of gigging. The next piece of information soon made me have a change of heart though. We had to re-record the backing track on the Tuesday, and for that, we were being given the use of the main live room and studio facility in *BBC Maida Vale*. I realised these moments didn't get offered up every day, and this was something that even I got somewhat excited over. I knew it would be some occasion, one to remember. Sure enough, it didn't disappoint.

When you're a kid and you dream of being in a recording studio, I think the perfect picture, as your imagination runs wild, is one somewhat similar to The Beatles being in *Abbey Road*, where they are gathered around little booths, and are being fussed over by sound technicians decked out in laboratory coats, overseen by a well-dressed gent with an accent like Terry Thomas, offering instruction from a control room akin to a spaceship, situated behind a glass panel, and overlooking the whole studio floor. It was indeed pretty much like those classic photographs from the 60s. George Martin and Phil Spector-esque. Certainly a completely different league to what we were used to. The studio's engineers also relished the opportunity to record a live session for an eight-piece band. Usually we would be greeted by heavy sighs and rolling eyes in such situations, but these boys couldn't get us set up quick enough. I recall this being the first session where I felt somewhere close to being competent on my instrument, but I didn't feel overawed or nervous by being put under the microscope in what could have been perceived as an intimidating situation. I knew my lines, and I was going to enjoy this unique experience of recording in one of the UK's most famed studio environments. It was over in a flash, probably less than two hours in total, and at least one of those was spent setting up, then dismantling our equipment. As you would expect, the *BBC* engineers were highly skilled and masterful. Getting the right live sound for a bunch of young Herberts from the Midlands was a breeze for them, but of course a privilege for us.

Our professional code of conduct didn’t stretch too far past the recording studio, and it wasn’t long before we were instigating mischief and mayhem. *The Beeb* had put us up in the *Tara Hotel* in Kensington, which was quite an upmarket affair at the time, and was certainly the first hotel I had stayed in that didn’t have a key system, but a touch card. These are obviously commonplace now, but then it felt like a scene from *Star Trek*. The clientele were mainly male business-types in suits, all very formal. On the evenings, we would always notice an influx of female guests, who tried a little too hard to fit in. They were classily attired, but it was apparent (to us anyway) exactly what their business entailed. The Suits ended up bankrolling our entertainment, as the call girls couldn't help but be distracted from their temporary employers by a gang of sprightly twenty-somethings strutting into the hotel bar. The staff at the *Tara* soon got hip to a potential mass hooker hi-jack, and made sure we were politely ushered away from the hotel disco on a nightly basis.

They probably had good reason to be suspicious of us, not least because Richard, our keyboard player, was rooming with Emo, our roadie for the duration of the stay, and every morning, unbeknown to Richard, Emo would wait until he had left the room, and then proceed to mess his bed up and smear jam and butter all over the sheets, while leaving one of Richard's favoured sordid publications open, and placed strategically on top of the carnage that would greet the maid every day upon her arrival to clean the room. Richard was an odd one though. As I mentioned before, his collection of magazines resembled something out of *Wrestling Monthly*, or gave hint to a sci-fi fixation. There was a lot of leather going on too, as I recall, not that I particularly paid close attention to his murky pastimes. What I do remember is that he would always get out of the shower cursing that he had ruined another set of underwear. He would appear from the bathroom dripping wet, and declaring "Shit! That's the third pair I've soaked this week!" He would simply forget to take his pants off before showering, and he actually used to wear boxer shorts over briefs. I questioned him as to why he did this. 'Extended foreplay' was his response ... Why the fuck anyone would have wanted to prolong any intimate action with Likiki (his Hawaiian name, remember?) is beyond me. He did used to make us laugh though; there was never a dull moment.

Most of the week was just spent hanging around. We were pitched against an operatic singer, a comedy duo called Waxy, a vocal trio whose name escapes me (but I know they did a fucking horrendous version of Huey Lewis and the News' *Power Of Love* on the show) and a kid called Matt Mudd, whose parents were in a late-Fifties vocal group called The Mudlarks, who had a novelty hit with a song called *Lollipop* in 1958. Everybody took the whole experience really seriously, and cue cards and sheets as thick as the *Magna Carta* were dished out, for all the acts to learn when and where the cameras would be focusing during the live recording. We used ours for roach card. Poor old Matt was torn between getting caught up in the Sharon Showbiz world of *Op Knocks* and falling into our camp of debauchery. He ended up getting chicken pox the day before the show was due to be filmed, so he had to postpone his fifteen minutes of fame. For the time being, anyway.

Chicken pox would have been a blessing for some of us; on the eve of our national television debut, me and Phil ended up getting ourselves arrested, and spent the night in Kensington nick. How this happened is somewhat of a blur, and seems ridiculously trivial now. I know it involved poppers (amyl nitrate) and a bicycle, and I certainly had my best night's sleep of that week bunked down in my cell. Phil still likes to tell me to this day how he sat perched on the edge of a toilet seat, listening to me snore myself into oblivion while hogging all the bed. Al Calnan, who was still looking after us (if that was even possible!) at the time, made a swift transformation into Bernie Rhodes mode, and hotfooted it down to *Kensington Police Station* to negotiate a way of getting us out in time for our appointment with Bob Monkhouse and the *BBC* the next day. Once the coppers found out we were bona fide prime time TV stars, their mood lightened, release forms were signed, and slaps on the wrist executed.

Our brief foray into TV-land was surreal and bizarre in equal measures. It was an early insight into how farcical and staged these prime time light entertainment shows really are. I imagine *The X Factor* and its ilk are no exception; the producers know already whom they want and will allow to progress. It's all rigged, pre-arranged, a con. I have no idea how we slipped through the net and were allowed to perform one of our original tunes on there. Maybe they were attempting to readdress the formula and add some credibility, which was ironic, as I thought we were damaging ours by agreeing to take part in the programme. What I do know for sure is that there was no way they were going to have us back on any subsequent shows.

The show's notorious host, Bob Monkhouse, only showed up on the Thursday afternoon for a dress rehearsal, and then the live show would be filmed on the Friday evening in front of a live audience, who were encouraged to clap, whoop and cheer for the acts they liked the most, which would be measured by a *Clapometer* for popularity. Just typing that thirty years later seems faintly ridiculous. From the off, there was tension and distance between our crew and Monkhouse. He was a household name back then, a darling of the *BBC* and our TV screens, a national treasure. We thought he was a relic, his humour naff and corny, so we could understand exactly why he replaced Hughie Green as the face of *Opportunity Knocks*. He was fucking weird, barely communicated with anyone while he was on set, and he sported a dazed, vacant expression as he wandered aimlessly around, constantly clutching a bottle wrapped in paper to conceal his poison. It was almost like he was on medication, such was his vague demeanour. He probably was, but the one thing that made him completely switch into life was the moment those cameras burst into action. He just totally transformed character and performed, as if he was battery-operated, and had an 'on' button for every time the TV studio went into transmission mode.

We had been sent a pre-planned set of questions that Bob would ask us on the couch after our performance. It was to be Hammy, Nick Reid and myself in the line of fire, huddled up next to Monkhouse. The questions were all fairly standard, predictable fare – Where do we come from? How long have we been together? What jobs do we have outside of the band? And so forth ... I felt we at least had to attempt to go off script somewhat at some point in the interview. In hindsight, we should have saved it for the recording on the Friday, but they would have just cut it out anyway, as the show didn't actually get broadcast until the Saturday evening, allowing them twenty-four hours to edit and tidy everything up, but we thought we'd chance our luck at the run through on the Thursday. Bob was orange; his skin looked unnaturally tanned, like a ripe satsuma. One of the scheduled questions enquired what our ambitions were. I loaded Hammy up with the answer. I had no idea if he was going to go through with it once we sat down beside Bob at dress rehearsals, or if he would bottle it, but I think I knew Hammy well enough by now ...

Bob – "So what is your ambition? What's the ultimate goal?"

Hammy – "To have a sun tan like yours Bob"

Ooh ... fuck me, if looks could kill! That quickly curtailed that interview, and off Bob retreated to his paper-covered bottle and dressing room, sending smoke signals back to the producer cursing these young upstarts who dared to attempt ridicule. A comic without a sense of humour. It was probably he that had me arrested that night.

Come the day of filming, nerves were jangling in some quarters, but most of our lot were all fairly relaxed. We were only miming after all, and the real graft was on Hammy's shoulders, but he took in his stride. He'd sung the tune a hundred times before in sweaty boozers, university halls etc., and a staged set with a few punters sat in front of us, and cameras pointing in our direction, still didn't really equate with the fact that there'd be approximately fourteen million people tuning in from the comfort of their living rooms the following night when it was beamed out by the *Beeb*. After all the week's build up it was pretty much over in a flash. Bob introduced us as Dance (how we would pronounce it) Stance (pronounced 'Starnce' how the Southern half of the country would) and off we went. We all posed brilliantly, pretending to tend proficiently to our instruments. Hammy was the star he always was, and then we found ourselves back on the sofa for a re-run of Bob's questioning. I sounded like a Brummie, Hammy spoke as if his voice hadn't yet broken, and Nick's contribution got edited down to a token sniff of his nose. We looked good though.

"Where are you playing next?" Bob enquired.

"*Mean Fiddler*", Hammy replied.

Bob – "Sounds like my agent ..."

... and so it went on, showbiz bollocks, forced, strained laughter, make it all about the host, he's the real star here ...

Our next task was to stand in a line while our popularity was measured by the *Clapometer*. Points were awarded according to how high the needle would reach in response to the applause of the studio audience, and then 0898 phone-voting added an interactive element once the show was aired. It was nothing short of embarrassing. The applause and reception for us in that studio was deafening. We actually broke the *Clapometer*. It registered off the scale, unprecedented. They had to ask the audience to do it again, with the same result. It was farcical. The producers doctored the result and outcome for the TV, and placed our reading at a lowly fourth place. I think a fucking juggling act fared better. I'm not sure we gave too much of a fuck as by then, as it was obvious to all that we wouldn't be returning for the finals, and neither would we have wanted to. We were harbouring no ambitions in that department; we just wanted to gain some national exposure.

The real triumph and festivities began when we arrived back in Atherstone on the Saturday the show was due to air. Our local pub, *Sweeties* (*The White Lion*), invited all and sundry to watch it live on their big screen, so most of the population of the town all piled into the pub (including the band) to celebrate our break into the big time. I was over the awkwardness of it all by now, and took it for what it was, a bunch of youths from a small working-class town having their fifteen minutes of fame. I didn't need to keep making excuses for it, all the locals thought we'd cracked it, and they were made up for us. We were local celebrities, at least for the rest of that week anyway. In the aftermath of TV-land we waited for our opportunity to come knocking upon our door. Even I thought we'd get some offers of work, or at least a few lines of enquiry. For what? I guess I'm not sure. We got one call off the back of it all, just one. One. *Rugby Bingo Hall* needed a turn to fill in for a cancellation a week on Friday, how were we fixed?

13 - IT WAS A VERY GOOD YEAR

1989. It was odd to be bidding farewell to the eighties. So much had happened, and it seemed like the decade would go on forever. It had heralded in the youthful exuberance of my teenage years, and was flickering out just as I adjusted to life as a young man without the love and guidance of a father. '89 felt better though, and a fresh wave of positivity swept through me. It had to; otherwise I would have been engulfed with anguish. 'Depression' wasn't a word that was employed; a 'state of melancholia' seemed more appropriate. Either way, I couldn't allow myself to be become dispirited.

The whole *Opportunity Knocks* farce still troubled me. While I felt I'd compromised my credibility, no one else gave a shit. It was done. History. What it did provide though was a financial lifeline for the band to continue for the next twelve months. It meant we could afford to return to the studio and keep a nine-piece group on the road. We played some momentous gigs that year, particularly in London. We virtually had a monthly residency at *The Mean Fiddler* up in Harlesden. It began by us filling it with coach loads of Atherstonians making the day trip out, but soon enough our nights there would sell out, with residents of NW10 and beyond in attendance.

Our great friend and mentor Al Calnan had made the move south too, uprooting from his flat in Sutton Coldfield to the bright lights, big city. He just took a punt, he was impulsive like that, and I admired him for it. He initially struggled to find suitable employment, so made ends meet by selling flowers to tourists outside *The Empire* on Leicester Square. Within six months he was firmly secured inside that famous old West End venue, managing the place. This of course was good news for us, as he would make sure Dance Stance were booked on a regular basis at their club nights. If memory serves correctly I think we used to mime, maybe with a live vocal (Hammy doing all the graft again). We'd only have to perform about three numbers as part of the "live" music attraction at DJ/club nights. I certainly remember that the stage rotated, and you'd start your set behind a curtain, facing the opposite way, and suddenly the stage would rotate to the left as the curtain opened. The punters looked as bemused as we did, to be faced by nine youths prancing about without their instruments plugged in. Fucking good money though.

With Al now decamped in The Smoke, we were partly fending for ourselves when it came to booking gigs and keeping band business ticking over. Our regular haunt in Atherstone was still the wine bar on Long Street, where Edwin Starr had spontaneously jumped up to perform with us. It wasn't a venue, it was far too small and intimate for that, but Baz and Jen the owners, and Yan before them, were music obsessives like ourselves. There was a good vibe about the place, and it was always busy no matter what day of the week you'd venture in. The food was tremendous too, probably one of the most underrated eateries we have ever had in Atherstone (with the exception of *Winnies*, *The Corner Caff* and *The Batch Bar* of course, but I'm talking high-end fodder here, frogs' legs 'n' all). Me, Hammy and Coddy were resident in there, it was like our office.

It was at the beginning of '89 when we first encountered a trio of business types, entrepreneurs who had started hanging out in the bar. They liked expensive champagne, red wine, steak, Bob Dylan, cricket, and most of all they liked conversation, usually about themselves, but they held court well. It was inevitable that our world would gravitate towards theirs. Ron and Melissa Goodyear were a husband and wife team, Dave was their stooge, and their racket was publishing. They'd had moderate success releasing written works by the likes of Ian Botham, Mike Read (the DJ), Uri Geller and a book of sketches by England wicket keeper Jack Russell. They were now looking to make a move into music publishing. We of course by now had a huge stockpile and back catalogue of songs; I suppose in theory it was a good match, and so the courtship began …

Initially we'd just see them in the wine bar and get inebriated with them, trading tales, usually music-related. The odd drunken proposal or promise would get dropped, but it was just idle chat for a while, and I think we were all cautious at first about jumping into bed with them (which I think they would have quite literally accommodated too). We were fiercely independent, and naturally suspicious of anyone who wanted a slice of our action. We knew Al, he was one of us, we trusted him implicitly, and before that our affairs had obviously been looked after by my dad, but these cats were a different breed to what we had been used to. I liked them; they were still old school, and there was a slight generation gap between them and our crew which, if anything, probably gave us an upper hand. To them we were young and hip. I could let modesty take hold here and discredit that judgment, but truth be told we were hip, kings of our own little castle, for a while anyway.

All that name-dropping malarkey has never impressed me, it's just hot air. If you want to win me over then action most certainly speaks louder than words. As if to prove their credentials and connections, Ron would start showing up with minor celebrities, or at least people whose names and reputations we knew. They even brought Uri Geller along to one of our meals at the wine bar. Not many Atherstonian folk know about that. We got wankered, and Hammy pestered him to bend spoons with his mind power. He didn't of course, but he did make some seeds grow in the palm of his hand. It could have been the vino playing tricks on us though.

We had a gig on local turf, a kind of DIY affair over at *The Old Liberal House* in Amington, which was as out in the country as you could imagine, but nevertheless rammed. I used to quite enjoy putting on these guerilla-style events in the middle of nowhere, as they felt unique and quite spontaneous. I recall this one in particular, as we made the rather bizarre decision to link the whole set together. Every song segued into the next without pause or interruption. I think it was almost certainly the result of being under the influence of the underground Go-Go scene that was unfolding in Washington and Detroit, via artists such as Chuck Brown and The Soul Searchers or Trouble Funk, who I'd just been to see at Birmingham's *Powerhaus* venue. I'm not so sure that our gelling of an hour and half of Dance Stance material had quite the same impact, but a bold and eccentric move anyway.

Ron, Melissa and Dave turned up unannounced with a guest in tow. He was dressed head to toe in black, sporting a beret and shades and a walking-cane (not for any aid may I add, just for the pose of it). He stood out from the crowd, a face, but not a face I instantly recognized. His name however, I was completely familiar with upon being introduced. It was the dandified Svengali, Justin De Villeneuve, who is probably best remembered for steering the career of Britain's first supermodel Twiggy. While touting his young protégée around fashion shoots in the sixties, De Villeneuve figured that the craft looked relatively simple, and subsequently set up his own photographic studio, soon discovering he had a natural talent behind the lens. He swiftly became responsible for capturing some of the most iconic images of the day, mostly of course featuring Twiggy, including the cover sleeve to David Bowie's *Pin Ups* album. During the 1970s he'd turned his attention to the music industry, and had success managing artists such as Lynsey De Paul and Clifford T. Ward. I think the Goodyears were circling around him to get involved in an updated and revised version of his (rather fantastic) memoirs, *An Affectionate Punch*, which had been published a few years earlier in 1986. I liked the guy; you couldn't help but be impressed. We drank till the early hours back in the wine bar *Small Talk* on Long Street. He too had a habit of name dropping, he liked to let you know that he knew the Krays, and would repeatedly steer their names into the conversation. He was still fairly connected within industry circles, and Ron sensed a way in for us.

A few weeks later, an idea that De Villeneuve had planted in the Goodyears' heads was presented to us. Scottish singer-songwriter Jim Diamond, who had just enjoyed enormous chart success with *I Should Have Known Better*, *Hi-Ho Silver* and *I Won't Let You Down* (under the guise of Ph.D.) had heard one of our old tunes *The Sweetest Pain* and saw great potential in it. He'd sent word via Justin that he would be interested in covering it for a future release. I'm not sure if it was naivety or stubbornness on my part (probably a bit of both), but instead of rubbing my hands at the prospect of an artist, who at the time sold thousands of records, showing an interest in recording one of our songs, I actually felt outraged, and became defensive. I figured that if Jim Diamond thought it was a hit then it should be us reaping its success and not him, plus I had absolutely zero respect for Jim Diamond either. I thought he was the fucking enemy, naff MOR bollocks, and I certainly didn't want him slaughtering one of our songs. Ridiculous of me really, but I'd conceded and compromised myself on the *Opportunity Knocks* debacle, so I guess I had my gloves up for a while, defending what I thought best for our corner. As I remember none of the other lads in the band opposed my outlook on this, and Hammy and Coddy were certainly as militant as I was.

With the benefit of thirty years' hindsight, I was wrong, too precious for my own good, and it certainly would have made everyone a payday in the long run. However, the lads knew I was well intentioned and principled, and most importantly they knew I had their backs. We were yet to sign any formal contract or agreement with Goodyears for them to represent us on a managerial basis. Terms were discussed soon after the honeymoon period which in theory I had no resistance to, but it was when we were informed that they just wanted to sign me, Hammy and Nick Read that I dug my heels in. I totally understood that they would probably only want to communicate and meet with no more than three of us, as we were a nine-piece band at the time, and that would obviously be chaos, but there was no way I was going to leave the other lads out of the loop and make them feel like session players or secondary members. We were a team, best friends, and I wasn't about to shit on them. After all, they'd just helped me through one of the darkest times of my life after the death of my dad, and we were like a band of brothers. It was standard practice to just have the main songwriters or focal points of any band signed to a binding contract, not all of the group, and in fact I probably did them no favours dragging them into it all, but they appreciated my unswerving loyalty, and it kept us a solid unit, equals. All for one, one for all. Ron finally relented and gave us what we wanted, which was for the entire band to scrawl their signatures onto the contract, even if he never spoke to them, which he didn't. It made them inclusive, and part of the deal. For the signing celebrations and PR photographs it was agreed that just the three of us would represent the band, so myself, Nick and Hammy were invited up to their manor, situated just up the road on the Leicestershire border in Orton on the Hill.

It was a boiling-hot Thursday afternoon at the height of summer, 1989. Everyone was dressed for the occasion and the cameras, suited and booted, Ron particularly flamboyant in a white suit, and his *Porsche* parked visible to all. They liked to make a statement. The house was magnificent, remote and secluded. You had to travel down to it via a path that stretched about a mile, winding into picturesque countryside. It was like being transported to a different century. Sunlight poured into the spacious living quarters through fine glass doors that opened out to reveal a delightful, typically English country lawn, the like of which I'd only really seen previously in magazines. It was a sight to behold for sure, especially on such a suitably glorious day. The soundtrack was a heavy rotation of Van Morrison's *Avalon Sunset* album and *Oh Mercy* by Bob Dylan. I recall them playing *Mandinka* from Sinead O'Connor's debut LP a lot too. They unleashed the biggest bottle of champagne I'd ever witnessed, the sort you see at the *Grand Prix*, and then tossed us a lump of solid to smoke, which was the size of a fucking house brick, and it wasn't even 2 p.m. yet. Time actually stood still for the remainder of that day, it was magical.

People came and went, and I couldn't work out if they were employees or just friends on a fleeting visit. I remember getting trapped in the kitchen, where I was accosted by a drunken but attractive lady, who was certainly old enough to be my mum, but had obviously kept herself in good shape, and judging by her enthusiasm for a tipple, liked to live the high life too (all of Ron's associates did). She was into spiritual healing, and proclaimed herself to be in touch with a higher connection from the outer world. All that nonsense bores the crap out of me, especially if the messenger is hammered on a couple of bottles of *Vino Collapso*. I get cornered for what seems like an eternity by this semi-coherent woman, who's now stroking my face, and telling me how much I remind her of an old boyfriend of hers. Predictably he died of a heart attack aged just 42, and she can feel his spirit channeling the room. I've been sent to her as a sign. I know exactly what signs I'm getting, and I'm not so sure I fancy it. Turns out she's only Lady Lee Middleton, otherwise known as Lee Everett, and the late and ex-boyfriend she's referring to, that my blonde quiff reminds her of, is only Billy Fury! She later made headlines when she married comedian and DJ Kenny Everett. I'm sure her intentions were to take me *Halfway To Paradise* and beyond, but I have to admit I was fairly intimidated by her, and made my excuses, retreating back to the madness of Ron and Melissa's smoke and champers afternoon rampage. It's certainly a day that has lived long in the memory. I think I cut my quiff off the very next day …

Our working relationship with the Goodyears didn't fare so well. The only gig they secured was a stint at Loughborough Town Hall. Everything else that year we booked ourselves. They did, however, get us some studio time to record new songs at *The Basement* premises, right in the heart of Soho, on Wardour Street. What could possibly go wrong? We didn't get off to the best start. While the equipment was being set up, and microphones set out to amplify all the gear, we gathered in the hospitality suite upstairs. The studio manager came up to introduce himself, offered us refreshments and enquired if we'd like any music putting on. "There's loads of Pretty Things vinyl over there", he enthused, pointing over to a stack of LPs resting in the corner of the room.

"Fuck that shit!" Hammy responded, not very tactfully, "Have you got any soul?" Unbeknown to us, the geezer was the drummer in The Pretty Things. One-nil down already.

Our session was booked for five days, but we ended up getting evicted after three. We made good progress, recording the bulk of four tunes in the first couple of days, so all was not lost, or at least so we thought. The studio engineer was a tall fella called Dave, who was really amicable. It was the boss, the Pretty Thing, who had it in for us from the off. He had a weird hairline, obviously thinning, but he had dyed what hair he did have left jet black, and then painted in his hairline with what looked like mascara. It was fairly bizarre, and of course we couldn't talk to him without our eyes gazing up to his noggin, and the more you try not to do something like that, the more you find yourself staring at it. Predictably we soon had a name for him, we called him *Painter Man*. Painter Man's patience was finally pushed to the limit when he arrived one morning to be greeted by the aftermath of a party we'd thrown the previous night in his hospitality suite. It had a huge glass window that overlooked the Soho streets below, so we'd just encouraged passers-by to join us for a spliff and a beer, and had ourselves a disco with more vinyl we'd located that was not just confined to titles by The Pretty Things. It was fairly chaotic, and in retrospect I can see why *Painter Man* was miffed, though I'm not sure it warranted us being thrown out of the studio.

As it transpired, Ron hadn't paid the deposit for booking the recording time anyway, which unbeknown to us was making *Painter Man* nervous, and he was right to have his reservations. Not only had Ron not stumped up any cash for the studio, we also had the hotel on our back about the pending bill. It wasn't too long before the whole pack of cards toppled, and it became clear that Ron and his Goodyear Associates were living a champagne lifestyle on a lemonade budget.

Baz and Jen at the wine bar no longer saw Ron, Dave and Melissa quite so regularly once they had racked up a hefty tab that was left unpaid. They decamped for a while down the road to hold their meetings with us in the *Red Lion*, and pulled off the same trick there: charm 'em, mount up a monthly tab and disappear. Even we had been smitten (and bitten) by their charm, grand plans and proposals. They certainly knew how to talk, but for all the grandiose conversations, promises and expectations, our deal with them amounted to nothing. Our relationship lasted no longer than twelve months, and it took all the weight and negotiating power of the *Musicians Union Legal Department* to free us from that contract. On reflection we wasted a year, but as the decade turned to 1990, a whole new scene emerged that re-connected us (me and Hammy for sure anyway) back to our modernist roots and values, and in turn the band quickly found their way again, albeit in a slightly different guise.

We seemed to employ a revolving chair on the keyboard seat, Dean Harvey (who we re-christened Brains for his resemblance to the *Thunderbird*) initially took over from Richard Ward and then several months later was replaced by Corky (Corin Birchall), I had a good solid friendship with both of these characters, I'll be forever grateful to Brains for rescuing me from a scene in Telford where somehow I'd got caught up in a Pink Floyd / Drug den nightmare……..

True Story... Late 80's - I was doing a gig in Telford. The gig was shit so we decided to cheer ourselves up by carrying on our evening and taking a visit to the local nightclub. They had never seen Quiffs and clean clothes in Telford. Girls fawned and flirted, Boys flexed and prepared for battle. We were in trouble. Sharp exit required. The Dean and I had to flee rapidly in his motor, a girl ushered us through a back door, our departure quickly rumbled we soon had a Lynch mob in hot pursuit, no time to pause the girl dived in our motor, Dean hit the gas, rocks hit our car, a gang baying for blood threw anything they could get their hands on at our vehicle as we sped away from Telford's nightlife as swiftly as we could.

Now... we couldn't just dump our female accomplice out into the street so being the courteous gents we were we offered her a lift home. Home however ended up being a half hour detour in the opposite direction to our homeward destination. She invites us in. We accept. Why? I really have no idea, we'd already had our fill. Shit gig, even shittier club, almost got our faces filled in, dodged rocks at an 70mph getaway chase... and still we weren't done! Oh the folly of youth.

So... we enter this house to be greeted by a scene from the living dead, in the living room, which is in complete darkness except for the Lights on the stereo blaring out, there's a group of about ten folk either nodding out or shooting up brown. Heroin. We're in a junk den. None of them either flinch or acknowledge our presence when we enter the room, the only thing they are locked into (apart the H) is the Stereo.
What's their soundtrack that keeps them in their trance? You got it.
The Wall by Pink Floyd.

Comfortably Dumb... it was time to escape. I felt it only right to say goodbye to the girl who routed our getaway, I walked into the kitchen to say farewell she grabbed a hold of me with one hand and lifted her skirt up with the other, I couldn't help but notice that she had neglected to put on any underwear..."you" she said "are staying here with me"
Oh fuck. I'm faced with *The Wall*, A Telford No Knickered Nympho and a house full of smack heads! "Run like Hell" indeed. Dean got the motor revved once again; they were too busy smoking rocks rather than throwing them this time though.

Mostly it was a frustrating period, but I cannot deny that it was a lot of fun too. I couldn't help but really like Ron, and he always filled you with great self-esteem and confidence, so his man-management skills weren't lacking. In our brief time together I did get to have dinner with Uri Geller, get pissed with Justin De Villenueve, be seduced by Billy Fury's ex, eat in the best restaurants, drink the finest champagne, record down in Wardour Street in the heart of Soho and receive a first draft of John Repsch's story of Joe Meek. I often wonder where Ron is now and what he's up to. Probably pulling off the same stunts somewhere else, either home or abroad. I couldn't help but admire him.

14 - I ALMOST MET A BEATLE

Having revealed little-known facts such as Uri Geller, Justin De Villeneuve, Geoff Hurst and Edwin Starr all spending evenings in Atherstone Town, I thought it only right that I should clear up an age-old Atherstonian folk tale that has gathered myth, misrepresentations and fabrications of the truth over the intervening years. I can tell you exactly what happened the night a Beatle came to town as, to quote Welsh comedian Max Boyce, I was there.

I have heard numerous variations, elaborations and discrepancies, which have only become more fanciful and ludicrous, especially with the ascent of the internet and social media. These have ranged from Bob Dylan, Tom Petty and Roy Orbison all being in attendance, to a full-on Beatles reunion in the *Star Tandoori Curry House*. So, it's only right that I take a quick detour and tell you the actual story as it really unfolded.

Atherstone was a busy and bustling town back in the late eighties. You could go out most nights, even in the week, and find the pubs rammed full of drinkers. At one point, you could almost fill your weekly calendar with social events. Wednesday was the disco down at *the Clock*, Thursday you could take your pick between *Grendon disco* (remember the trouser incident) or the *Football Club* disco (remember the mods 'n' rockers altercation). Fridays and Saturdays took care of themselves, as the streets would be lined with folk, every pub packed, and lord knows we had enough of them (Atherstone was famed at one time for having more Public Houses within a space of so many square miles than any other town of its size in the country). Sunday, either *the Legion* would put a DJ on, or you could venture just up the road to Fenny Drayton where the village boozer, *The Royal Haven*, would be in full swing. Mondays, *Bertie's* would run a club night coupled with cheap drinks, then Tuesday would pretty much be the dead night, when everyone recouped and recharged, ready to go again on the Wednesday. The following occurred on a Tuesday night, the recovery evening. No-one was out.

Jeff Lynne of ELO fame had been a regular in *the Red Lion* on Long Street for the best part of a year. Nobody batted an eyelid, as not that many folk realised who he was. He had been out of the limelight for a few years, and it was almost uncool to admit to digging the Electric Light Orchestra around this period, their ship having long sailed. I think he enjoyed drinking anonymously in a tiny snug bar in Atherstone, and certainly no one bothered him in all the time I saw him pitched at the bar. We were on nodding terms. He knew that I knew, and we simply exchanged the odd hello. I find that quite unusual now, looking back upon it, as I am normally one to bowl over and strike up a conversation, but I thought it was obvious that what he liked about coming into town was the fact that he wasn't being hassled by anyone. Just an ordinary punter like everyone else. His regular night was a Sunday, almost every week for about 12 months.

Myself and Hammy knew the youth that lived there, Adam White, whose parents ran the hotel. He was into music, was a musician himself, a decent guitarist, and he had auditioned for The Pretenders at one point. He was slightly older than us, but we shared a passion for all things pop, soul, rock 'n' roll … Hammy's folks had *the Cricketer's Arms* pub on the Market Square at this time, and Adam knew we always hung out. If you phoned my house and I was in, then Hammy would be there too. If you called *the Crick's* and asked for Hammy, it also meant that I'd be with him. Tuesday evening the phone rang at the *Cricketer's*, and Ita, Hammy's mum, answered. It was Adam, asking if Sheas and Hammy were about; we were. Hammy picked the upstairs phone up. Adam was breathless with excitement; he could hardly get his words out....

"You're never gonna believe who's here in the pub?" he blurted out.
"Jeff Lynne?"

"Well … yeah! But you're not gonna believe who he has with him!"
Try us.

"George Harrison!"
I must admit it was quite impressive, a real living Beatle in Atherstone, in *the Red Lion* ... with Jeff Lynne... on a Tuesday night. Adam was beside himself, and urged us to dash round to the pub soon as we could. This was history! A Beatle!

Hammy being Hammy had to get himself changed first and roll a joint, so that probably took the best part of forty minutes or so. We arrived at *the Red Lion* to find Adam in all of a fluster. I'm not even sure he had yet mustered up enough confidence to approach them, and his folks owned the bloody pub. He was full of anxious, nervous excitement, and had called upon us for back up. The problem now was that they had just moved on, but all was not lost, as they had only decamped a few doors down to the local Indian restaurant, *The Star Tandoori*.

"Come on, quick!" cried Adam. "We need to go round now, and get a table". Now somewhat unbelievably, viewing this retrospectively decades later, both myself and Hammy thought this was a really naff idea. We sit in an Indian restaurant, on a dead Tuesday night in Atherstone, gawping in awe at George Harrison, who's enjoying a catch up with his old mate Jeff Lynne. We will look like dickheads. What are we going to say anyway? Not cool.

Adam was undeterred. "Sod you two then, I'm going round, I can't miss this opportunity." Off he went, One chicken Balti, a Beatle and *Mr Blue Sky*. In doing so, I can categorically say, despite all the imaginative, fanciful and extravagant tales that have passed into Atherstone folklore over the intervening years, that Adam White, to my knowledge anyway, was the only person apart from *the Star Tandoori* staff that met a Beatle that infamous night in Atherstone.

I can't believe we passed on it. Me and Hammy could have been Travelling Wilburys...

15 - NEIL, FRIEND OF THE STARS / SUPERSTAR DJ

The record shop hustle was gathering pace by the end of the decade. By 1989, the shiny new format known as *Compact Disc* was here to stay and was no longer suspiciously viewed as a fad. As a result, people actually started to dismantle their vinyl collections and traded them in, or sell them off to fund the new space-saving digital revolutionary option. It was boom time behind the counter. With sales figures up, and record companies desperate to break their artists, the album and singles reps out on the road and calling on our stores would pull off any stunt, or ply you with bribes to get catalogue numbers or barcodes through the chart registration machines that we had in our shops. These were compiled at the end of every week by a company called *Gallup*, who then in turn published the national chart, the *Top 40* being the holy grail of credibility and gratification for the record execs.

I was more than happy to help with hype. In return, I was showered with free records, CDs, T-shirts, complimentary tickets to gigs, and sometimes, best of all, corporate events that the labels staged for signing parties for new acts, or playback/listening dos for new albums, with meet-and-greets for the artists thrown in. Free drink flowed, and no-one really gave a fuck about what band or singer was on parade; it was about the piss-up. I loved these events. Rubbing shoulders with C-list pop stars and getting tanked up on free alcohol, I was in my element. I attended hundreds of them, from Crowded House's signing party for *EMI* on Harley Street in London, to Mirage miming their *Jack Mix '88* (Remember that? Thought not) in a backstreet nightclub in Birmingham. I found myself embroiled in the most bizarre situations during these shindigs. Sharing a bowl of chips with Basia, talking shoes with Martin Fry, karaoke with Bonnie Tyler, spliffs with UB40, a piss-up with The Pasadenas and throwing chicken drumsticks at Lenny Kravitz ...

I was never backwards in coming forwards in those days. I loved a bit of showbiz gossip, and would comfortably sidle up to whoever was being celebrated and befriend them for the night. More often than not I got on with them, probably because I was so obsessive and passionate about music that I always found common ground or a reference point to chat about. Most musicians are the same. Get them fired up talking about what inspires them and what they are listening to and you're up and running.

I didn't get quite so wankered in the presence of artists that I had respect for, as I genuinely didn't want to look a dick or talk shite to them. Jazzie B of Soul II Soul was as intelligent, engaging and cool as I'd hoped he'd be. Don and David Was (Was not Was) were impeccable and impressive gentlemen; I actually saw them play Leicester Polytechnic to literally our crowd who had been invited via the record label, probably no more than 30 folk, and they treated the gig as if it was a packed arena, played a 90 minute set that was a killer, and proceeded to invite the whole audience backstage after the show for drinks.

I would find myself in the most salubrious of settings and the most unlikely situations at times, like *Royal Box* hospitality for The Rolling Stones at *Wembley Stadium*. It was the *Steel Wheels* tour, and the whole of *Sony Music* turned out en masse to sip on free champagne and complimentary cocktails. Almost everybody who was signed to *CBS/Sony* at the time was there (with the noted exception of Sade unfortunately), and predictably, I took full advantage of the refreshments on offer, and proceeded to instigate my own mischief. I'd taken to the awful habit of urinating up the leg of semi-recognizable artists that didn't meet my criteria of credibility, and in the space of a few months, I'd been known to piss on the trouser legs of Guy Chadwick from The House Of Love, The Wonderstuff's Miles Hunt, and now, with the rather plush backdrop of *Wembley's* royal enclosure, I homed in on my next victim. I should hasten to add that this all took place in the Gents' toilets, I didn't just randomly start pissing up people's legs; that would just be a step too far ... So, I'm relieving myself in the toilets of *Wembley's* VIP lounge at the Rolling Stones tour party, and who should walk in and sidle up next to me at the urinals but *Epic Records*' new pop pin-up poster boy Halo James. Now Halo (I think his name was Christian, and the band were known as Halo, but that's just minor detail) was undeniably a pretty-looking young fella with a generous amount of fair hair that was styled into a quiff, not too dissimilar to my own do of the time. I had in fact been the recipient of numerous taunts over the previous few months stating that I resembled Mr. James here, so I seized my moment – "Hey up Halo! Everybody reckons I look like you", I declare, before firing piss all up his leg. How I never got a thump for all of this, or ejected from the building, is beyond me. I guess it's Rock 'n' Roll of a sort … I'm glad to report that my rather shameful 'fascination with urinating over pop stars' phase soon passed.

Some of my favourite and most memorable nights out courtesy of record company hospitality arrived when David Bates, head honcho at *Phonogram Records*, re-launched the *Fontana* Label, and decided to promote and celebrate this with a series of concerts by his featured artists at the legendary *Town & Country Club* in Kentish Town, North London. I, along with my co-workers from the record shop, attended several of these showcases. The evenings always ended with a gathering in the upstairs bar at the venue, where (free) drink flowed and B-list/C-list celebrities would gather. My good friend and fellow record-counter colleague Bess would always be aiding and abetting my mischievous behavior. She was quite incorrigible too, so we made a formidable team. She was the first person to play me *Hang Ups* by T-Rex, and we got on instantly. I didn't need much motivation when it came to getting my kicks, but Bess always ramped up the fun factor when we went out, and she was a constant sidekick for most of these record company shenanigans. It was she who during this period referred to me as "Neil, Friend Of The Stars". It's a shame that Insta-photos captured on mobile phones weren't the currency back then, as I'd have some corkers. I guess on reflection it is probably best that there isn't any photographic evidence.

Fontana and David Bates hosted monthly affairs featuring the aforementioned House of Love, newcomers Andy Pawlak, Love & Money, and even Swing Out Sister did a showcase. The real big event that drew in a minor celeb count was when Was (not Was) played at the *Town & Country Club*. It was a far cry from a few weeks previously, when we had been witness to the sparsely-attended show in Leicester. Their headline slot in London was rammed, and I was pleased for them. They deserved it. A great live band.

At the reception in the bar post-gig, I was fairly sober. As I said previously, if I respected a band or artist, I conducted myself in a more appropriate manner. As I made my way through the crowd upstairs, Bess pointed out Tears For Fears co-founder and bass player Curt Smith, who was busy holding court, entertaining a bevy of what can only be described as Supermodels, all gathered round and hanging on his every word. Now, I can't really claim to be a fan as such, but I did quite respect them, and thought that the last couple of Tears For Fears albums were actually alright. Somewhat unusually for this period (1989), it had been ages since their last record, which was the globally successful album *Songs From The Big Chair* (1985, so four years to be precise). Of course, once Bess had spotted him, I just couldn't help myself making a beeline in his direction.

"Oh, hello ... Curt isn't it?" – He loved being recognized in front of his adorning beauties …

"So, what's going on with the band and the new record? It's been a while …"

Now, our Curt is quite a tall fella; he certainly had some height over me anyway, so as I join his social circle of perfectly formed females, he rolls his tongue around his cheeks, peers down from his lofty perch, and transforms into the most boastful, pompous bore. He uses my line of enquiry into his music to vainly impress his flock.

"Well, we went to Eddy Grant's studio out in Barbados, but it didn't quite work out there, so we took some time-out in the Caribbean. We shot a couple of videos … relocated to try out George Martin's place in Montserrat … that didn't quite pan out … headed over to the States ..." Zzzzzzzzzz!

On and on he went, name-dropping destinations, producers, locations … It was a total bore-off from a complete show-off. I let him ramble on, just waiting to seize my moment ... He finally finished his overbearing, tedious monologue by uttering the words "So, hopefully it will be with you sometime around the end of summer".

I couldn't help myself. "Great", I finally replied, "Well, I hope it's better than the last pile of fucking shit you brought out!" I turned swiftly on my heels and made my way to the bar before he had a chance to respond. His (perfectly chiselled) jaw hit the floor, and the female accompaniment did their best to suppress their laughter. Ironically, come that September, *Sowing The Seeds Of Love* found some heavy rotation on my sound system, but I never regretted putting pretty-boy Curt in his place for his pop star charade.

My newly discovered hedonistic vigour, coupled with an unquenchable zest and passion for music, led me to having the bright idea of turning my hand to a spot of DJ-ing. I'm not quite sure what sparked all this off, but I've always wanted to share my enthusiasm. I wouldn't be one to keep to myself the discovery of a new tune or band that thrilled me. I'd want to tell the world, and turn folk onto new sounds. I am still like that now. The idea of putting on our own events to spin tunes as a musical social gathering appealed to me. There's no way I would get into doing weddings and parties, as if it was a job, I had to make these events happenings, to appeal to the right crowd, where my intentions, and most importantly the music I was playing, would be appreciated. Inevitably, I roped Hammy in. I'd play the tunes whilst he would MC, and act as host and compère. Of course, his involvement wouldn't come without colourful intervention and ridiculous ideas.

Initially, we used our regular haunt, *The Wine Bar* on Long Street, but after our first couple of events, the nights proved to be so popular that it was obvious we needed not only a bigger venue, but also somewhere that would keep an intimate vibe to the proceedings. *Sweeties*, or to give it it's official moniker *The White Lion*, was the main pub in Atherstone, another drinking establishment that felt like a second home to lads and ladies of my age. It was a good boozer, steeped in tradition, but always up for trying something new. It had experienced a whole host of really great landlords over the years (including Mr Sweet), and our little foray into clubland coincided with a very amicable fella called Bob Broadhurst, who was the current tenant of the pub when we turned up with our decks and piles of vinyl records. He didn't need any coaxing; he knew his pub would be packed, and all of our crowd were big drinkers, who frequented the boozer anyway. With Hammy in tow, it was never quite as simple as just playing a few records in the corner of the pub. As always, he would need to take proceedings a step further, which during our stint at *Sweeties* included dressing up as *Batman & Robin*, eating chunks of solid hash that made me feel like I was entering a dark cave every time I put my headphones on to cue up a record, telling anyone that asked for a tune who we didn't approve of to fuck off, and lifting the needle off records (my records!) that bombed (people didn't dance to), and flinging them across the pub like Frisbees. We caused so much chaos and mayhem that they had to employ a minder to stand by the DJ decks, although I can't recall anybody ever complaining. It was all in the name of Showbiz, and the pub was always rammed.

I really quite embraced our first foray into DJ-ing, and putting on nights where I could share my infatuation for whatever music I was digging at any given time. During this period I would have almost certainly been airing a mix-up of obscure 70s soul and funk records, re-branded for the next generation as rare groove, and a smattering of hip hop, which was seeing a huge resurgence, and had become fascinating again, via the samples the artists were using. Then I would throw in the odd house track. I found the dance music emanating and emerging from the States quite exciting, and we were importing a fair bit via the record shop, so I had been fortunate to be privy to records like Raze's *Break 4 Love*, and Frankie Knuckles' *Tears*. A lot of my old soul boy cohorts were turned off, but I saw that whole scene as an extension of a tradition dating back decades, with Black American urban music being embraced in the UK and interpreted for a whole new culture and scene. It was nothing particularly new, just a hip modification of something that started with the first rock 'n' roll singles being played in cafés and on jukeboxes, then onto the early influx of soul sides via labels like *Tamla Motown*, *Stax*, and the blues label *Chess*, that commanded crowded dancefloors in the all-night bars and dancehalls of the 60s. And so it goes on …

Our residency at *Sweeties* was confined to once a month, and I was keen to expand on this and do more. I think Hammy saw it as a bit of a novelty, a bit of fun, and a drink-up each month. He didn't so much lose interest, but thought it would be far more entertaining to be the other side of the DJ booth dancing and being a social barfly, something at which he undoubtedly excelled.

The rules for pub opening hours had just changed, which made a radical difference to how people distributed their social and drinking activity. Previously pubs could only serve alcohol between the hours of 12 p.m. to 3 p.m., then re-open for the evening shift at 6 p.m., before calling last orders at 11 p.m.. You had to strategically plan your lock-ins after the bell for last orders rang. We take for granted now being able to get served at pretty much any hour you wish. I do believe the restrictions made drinking more appealing. It was like a sport, and for a while, I was pretty good at it too. Most of the folks in my town were, to be fair, and I think at one point Atherstone had the most pubs per square mile in the UK for a place of its size and population. The streets would be lined with bodies (some still standing!) come the weekends, and even weekday quaffing dragged the numbers out. The pub was a social hub, and very much part of the fabric of our community. I'd noticed a significant shift in habits after the licensing hours changed. Beforehand, you would always know where certain people would be at what time, where they would start, and where they would end up on their sessions.

Everyone had their own little route, but once the timings turned into a free-for-all, patterns altered, and it became more difficult to predict where folk would be, and what were the best bars in which to see a certain crowd at a certain time. I know this sounds radically implausible now, but hey... we didn't have mobile phones back then. Communication came from talking, making prior arrangements and all that. We couldn't just send a text message or call to see where the action was at.

Sunday afternoon socials were always big on the weekly agenda, an unwind after the comedown of a Friday and Saturday, and the last walk-out before the Monday morning blues beckoned. It gave me an idea. A Sunday afternoon DJ session where everyone could gather, a place where you'd guarantee like-minded guys 'n' gals all under one roof, with the addition of me in the corner of the pub, spinning some tunes to suit the atmosphere. My dear old mate Pete Martin suggested we could host a session for a few hours (12 p.m. until 4 p.m.) in the back room of *the Angel* pub, situated by the church on Atherstone's Market Square. Pete thought it would be a good idea to run it like a music club, where people brought tunes, albums, singles etc. that they had been listening to, and we could run it as a social jukebox, with me hosting it and airing the songs. Swapping tastes and ideas related to music. It appealed to me. So that's how it began. For about 2 weeks...

There are certain moments that have gained honorary entry into Atherstone's folklore, like *Winnie's Cafe* opening at night as the pubs were turning out, and "erotic" dancers in the window of the *Three Tuns* on the middle of Long Street. My discos in *the Angel* undoubtedly qualify for such a lofty accolade. The music club concept just couldn't last. Beer was being consumed (in great quantities), spirits were high, people just wanted to dance ... and so it soon turned into a monster! An all-day Sunday session. Twelve p.m. kick-off, and bop till you drop. The official kicking-out time on a Sunday evening was 10.30 p.m., but we rarely adhered to that, and we wound it up somewhere between 11.00 p.m. and midnight. I'd witness people come out at midday, initially fresh and ready for an afternoon social, get absolutely hammered by 4 p.m., head home, get a couple of hours' kip, then come back out at 7 p.m. to re-join the party. We also had a day-shift posse and regular night-timers, as well as the hardcore bunch that would see it through all day. Of course, I was one of these too, as I was the host, DJ, compère and chief fucking piss-head. All my drinks were free. No money exchanged. Whatever I wanted, when I wanted, a free bar, from 12 p.m. to 12 a.m. Good job I was in my prime, as it was something of a marathon. Ten hours plus of tuneage too, which in theory could have become hard to cater for and provide a variation each week, but I never struggled to mix it up. I played anything that took my fancy. From pop to punk, indie to funk, disco, reggae, rock 'n' roll. Anything went. It all fitted perfectly. No rules.

It (and I) was fairly hedonistic for the times, which seemed suitable enough as we steered and geared our way through the mid-90s. I had these fairly out-there ideas some weeks, which would range from getting the local barber in and tossing a coin to see if the professional here would cut your hair, or in the event of a wrong call ... me. Pissed. High. Armed with scissors. Then we had a cracker-eating competition - see how many dry *Jacob's* crackers folk could ram into their mouths and swallow in one minute. I think a bucket was required for that one. When we were oversubscribed with male drunks, I would encourage them. I held arm-wrestling tournaments. All this while people carried on dancing to the tunes. You could smoke in pubs then too. Unthinkable now, but not only could you smoke, we smoked weed (and solid) too. You must have been able to smell the gaff from miles away, but no one bothered us. On the contrary, folk flocked from neighbouring villages and towns. We had ourselves a reputation. Well ... more to the point, I did.

Only once, I remember getting a visit from the local constabulary. They came in plain clothes, far too plain. It was a dead giveaway. We'd had a tip off anyway of the Sunday they were due to drop by, so I'd requested that the smoking be knocked on the head for the session, as we'd risk getting shut down. Two couples turned up, two males and two females. They did their best to mix in with the crowd, but it was ridiculously obvious that they were straights and Old Bill too. I think they took one look at the place, the atmosphere, the sounds, the spirit of the people, and just knew it was all well-intentioned fun, and they enjoyed it. Even when I played the theme tune to *The Sweeney*, and everyone got on the chairs and tables and chanted the melody to them.

It was a funny, riotous old time. We lasted a long time too, three whole years. I even gave up my job in 1996, as the landlord paid me more for a Sunday afternoon than I could earn all week at the record shop. It was gloriously nuts and yes, I was the ringleader and the catalyst for the ideas, but you needed the right people to make it work, and Atherstone has always excelled at joining in with a party. It was probably the peak of indulgence for a golden generation of 24-hour party people. We timed our shebang to perfection.

Of course, it couldn't last, and it was fairly miraculous to make it past the first couple of years. I personally had the best of times, as I am sure many other people attending did too, but I simply had to rein in my indulgences. It was only going to end one way, and the trick to leaving something truly memorable behind is to realise when the party is over. Thankfully, I got my timing just about right. I cleaned up, and decided it was high time I reconnected to my modernist roots …

16 – EVERYTHING I DO WILL BE FUNKY FROM NOW ON

As the decade turned, so did our tastes, and inevitably the nineties heralded changes. Musically, I suppose it will mostly be remembered for brit pop (Oasis, Blur etc.) and shit pop (Spice Girls, Take That etc.) but in the decade's formative years there was plenty of cultural activity occurring, especially in the underground.

I don't like to dwell on the "M" word too much these days; it's been hi-jacked, the needle appears to be stuck in the same tired groove, free forward-thinking replaced by fancy dress parties. Frowns would form, and scorn be poured upon any individual who would dare to challenge the parameters now, but once upon a long ago, it was a very different modern world that I'd heard about. I was baptised in a broad church, and never was the modernist movement more in full bloom than around 1991, when it transformed, all bright and beautiful, into a whole new development. Once again, clothes and music held hands, as is the case with all great youth cultures, and the indications were clear at the end of the 80s, with the resurgence of obscure funk and soul records via the rare groove happenings. But this time around it would not revolve around a scene that was purely rooted in the past. Feet were firmly planted in the present.

The Duffer of St. George, then a tiny shop premise in the heart of Soho on D'Arblay Street, was a kind of epicentre of cool. Well, to me it was anyway. I'd save up for weeks, make regular trips on the train down to London whenever I could, and buy up the latest *Duffer* cardigans, or maybe a new jacket. Trainers were big on the shopping agenda too, and around this time I'd got myself a bit of an addiction collecting old-school *Puma* and *Adidas*, even getting them imported (pre-internet remember). Actually, I vividly recall driving down Coleshill Road in my hometown of Atherstone and seeing a young girl probably about 14/15 years old, with short-cropped bleached blonde hair, white *Levis*, and on her feet (the killer ...) *Adidas* shell-toes with green stripes! Red? OK. Black? Sure. But green? How? I almost crashed my car; I was so gobsmacked at witnessing such a cool young whippersnapper stealing some thunder on my doorstep. How could she possibly know? She must have fluked that look I concluded, but it was worn with too much effortless suss, savvy, style and cool to be unintended. Hmm … we'll come back to her later in my story.

Musically, two labels were quick to provide the perfect soundtrack, two labels independent from commercial pressure, free to release and make records that they loved and believed in. You came to trust these labels, like a British *Tamla Motown* or *Stax*. Nearly everything they released for the first two years of existence was worth checking. *Acid Jazz* and *Talkin' Loud* led the way in the early 90s: they set the scene. While some records have stood up well from this golden period, others have proved to be of their time, but it's important to acknowledge that this was about the present moment, it was about taking the best elements of what had gone before and shifting it forward, doing something creative, fresh and new. It was the ultimate style adrenaline rush for me, modernism personified, for a while. I'd be at a JTQ gig and get a tap on my shoulder, only to be asked about my trousers. Turned out the young Indian hipster making the enquiry was the trousers' tailor, Ravi Schmee. It was a time of enterprise, young clothes designers, rappers, musicians, record labels, DJs etc. … anything seemed possible. I remember those days as being full of optimism and positivity. Two records stood out by a country mile. I loved them. I still do. *Road To Freedom* by The Young Disciples and *In Pursuit Of The 13th Note* by Galliano. If either of these records were released tomorrow, they would still sound fresh and vital: a timeless quality.

I had no choice but to alter the course of my own ship. I was fully engaged, engrossed and enthused by all that was briskly unfolding, and it was time to shake up my own band too. Dance Stance was synonymous with the previous decade, our pubescent youth, and finding our feet. I think we were all ready and equipped for a new challenge. Almost everybody stayed on board, and we re-invented ourselves as Rare Future (I know, another terrible name, but the drink and narcotics were taking a hold by this time). Soul was always our bag, so there was no bandwagon jumping; things just got a little funkier, that's all, and by now we could all play, and our reputation as a solid, tight unit just took a giant leap forwards. Heavyweight Super Funk. What ensued for the next three or four years were some of the happiest times of my musical journey. We gigged constantly, working our way into clubs that had funk nights on, meaning a tailor-made full house that would appreciate what we were about.

I know I have probably made it sound like one big party and to a degree it was but we did also take our craft seriously and have pride in our creativity. It was around this time that we engaged in two very fruitful recording sessions, one down at the *Acid Jazz* studios and HQ situated on the old *Tin Pan Alley* in Denmark Street, London where decades previously The Rolling Stones had frequented to capture their early work, we almost signed with Eddie Piller at *AJ* around this period, he dug the sessions we'd done but I think their roster and release schedule was cemented for the next 12 months so nothing materialised in the end.

We also played in front of an audience for a live broadcast on *BBC Radio 5*, I heard it recently and was surprised at how tight and accomplished (and funky) we sound. This line up now included future Stone Foundation Conga Player Rob Newton as well as Myself, Phil and former SF sax Gary Rollins, our history consistently entwines. As ever, with anything myself and Hammy were involved in, we couldn't just have a normal night out. Even when touring with the band, incidents would just occur, scenarios would unfold, and future stories would be written.

We carried a colourful crew and entourage around that time too. A guy called Jeff Brampton drove for us, probably because he was the only person we knew who owned a van. We liked his company too. And his weed. He would consume it via a homemade bong that resembled a recorder. It was blue, and made a high-pitched whooping noise as you pulled upon its contents. It was christened the *Blue Flute*. Jeff had legendary house parties too. He lived in a flat above the local bakery, and I remember being so spaced-out at one of his shindigs that I sported a hollowed-out loaf of *Hovis* on my head all night (maybe that's a hat I could resurrect in the future?) Jeff's driving habits were never straightforward either; he had a siren and a flashing light which he would place on top of his van when we encountered traffic on the motorway, and just pull into the highway maintenance lane to skip past all the queuing traffic. We never got stopped or fined once. Jeff's real moment of glory though came via an unforgettable occasion at a gig in Derby. The more we ceased chasing attention and record industry interest, the more we drew people to our thing. As a live band, we were undeniably something of a tour de force; it was an enjoyable group to be part of, and our enthusiasm for playing must have been infectious, as the gigs were always, without fail, a joyous celebration. Word soon got out. The club promoters and venue booking agents started to take note, and prestigious support slots became available. We toured with Roy Ayers, The Crusaders, Average White Band, James Taylor Quartet, Mother Earth. We even opened up for George Melly at a festival once - he was a real character.

Of all the engagements, the one we were most thrilled to secure was supporting Gil Scott-Heron on the three Midlands dates of his UK tour. We were massive fans, I owned virtually every record he had ever released, and it was a big thing for us. We were all fully aware that by this point in his life Gil was facing his own demons, and was experiencing a battle with both drug and alcohol abuse. He wasn't in great shape. The gigs however, still never failed to connect. His talent, genius and songs carried him through every night. His band were on the money too. Tragically, though, it was a sorry sight to witness Gil's personal fall from grace, such a principled, intellectual and gifted individual ravaged and compromised by addiction. In Leicester, I brought some of my LPs for him to sign, only to be told that it wasn't worth risking defacing them, as he had a habit of just scribbling on them, so they stayed in my bag.

Our last night opening for Gil was in Derby, at an intimate but funky little venue called *the Warehouse*. It was the height of summer, temperatures were soaring, and the place was a sweatbox. After we finished our set, we decided to watch Gil from the side of the stage, where there was a fire exit door leading outside. The band appreciated the ventilation, so didn't mind us gathering there for a vantage point. Midway through his performance, Gil strolled over in our direction and took a moment to cool down, while Kim, his keyboard player, performed a solo. Gil is really tall, not that this has any real bearing on the story, but I thought I'd tell you anyway. Even in his delicate state of balance he was an imposing figure, tall, lean, all skin and bone. Then of course there was THAT voice, the very same pronounced tone that you have heard recall countless tales via his recordings, tales of *Winter In America*, tales of *Whitey On The Moon*, tales of *the Revolution not being televised....* Well, in Derby, that voice spoke to us - "Hey man, that a joint you got cooked?" Gil Scott-Heron asks Jeff Brampton. Jeff had indeed just loaded up a spliff the size of a coach exhaust, and was more than happy to pass it Gil Scott-Heron's way. We made small talk about both the gig and the stifling heat, while Gil got greedy on Jeff's joint. I'm sure he let Kim Jordan extend her solo by sixteen bars while he made the most of our hospitality.

What unfolded next was one of those surreal moments that seem to happen in slow motion. Gil Scott-Heron passed the joint back in Jeff's direction. In Gil's other hand, he was clutching a towel, to wipe away the beads of sweat trickling down his forehead. The spliff needed re-igniting. Jeff had one of those brass *Zippo* lighters, the ones where you can adjust the size of the flame. As Gil turns to walk back onto the stage and re-join his band, he tosses his white towel over his shoulder, doing this at the precise moment that Jeff flicks his lighter to fire up the joint. Jeff's Zippo is set to flame-thrower mode; he has it on the most extreme setting, kicking out a huge flame, which with impeccable comedic timing catches the corner of Gil's towel … just as he's walking back out onto the stage.

Time stops. It's like someone has pressed the pause button. All of us are just rooted to the spot, jaws on the floor, as we watch Gil make his entrance back onto the stage with flames billowing behind him. I break our silence - "Jeff ... you've just set Gil Scott-Heron on fire ..." Fucking hell! Jeff finally springs into action and chases after him, patting out the flames from the burning towel. Thankfully, Gil is so stoned that he doesn't really have a clue what's going on. He just perches himself down at his piano as Jeff whips away his towel, and then proceeds to play like Les 'fucking' Dawson for the next five minutes... I always wonder what it must have looked like if you were stood out front in the audience. Gil Scott-Heron casually walking back out from stage right ... on fire... followed by Jeff Brampton banging flames out on his back. I've told this story to friends who I'm sure either don't believe me or think I'm grossly exaggerating. Then a few weeks later, we'll be out, Jeff will walk in and I'll say "Hey! This is my mate Jeff who set fire to Gil Scott-Heron." What an amazing accolade to carry through life, eh?

It was no coincidence that this period saw the triumphant return of our modernist mentor, Paul Weller. After spending some time away from the public glare in the aftermath of the eventual demise of The Style Council, Weller took tentative steps back into the live arena armed with a clutch of new songs. The initial shows went under the guise of The Paul Weller Movement. Even that excited me, as it was a nod to *Stax* legend Isaac Hayes. Subsequently, Paul has kind of distanced himself, or been dismissive of those couple of years re-treading the boards and rekindling his love affair with music. I can understand and appreciate why, as it must have felt like starting all over again for him, but I can categorically declare that from a fan's perspective it was exhilarating. First up, he was playing at small university halls or intimate club venues, so it was a rare and unique opportunity to see him up close and personal again. The new songs, which were pretty much the basis of his first self-titled solo album, were incredible, informed by a mix of influences and stylings ranging from Traffic and Spooky Tooth to soul, jazz and funk.

Early on in the formation and ascendancy of Paul's solo years he decided to stage a series of consecutive gigs around London. I attended four nights on the bounce, at the *Town and Country Club 2*, *the Clapham Grand*, *the Mean Fiddler* in Harlesden and *Subterania*. I went with my mate Billy Butlin (another nickname of course, but a straightforward one for me to come up with, as his surname was actually Butlin, so Dean became Billy, after the famous red coat). The gigs were insanely exciting, and there was even a brief Style Council reunion at the first date when his then wife Dee C Lee and Mick Talbot jumped up on stage for an impromptu session. As Billy and I arrived in the borough of Highbury and Islington to make our way across to the *Town and Country Club 2*, an old-age pensioner shuffled past us who I thought I recognised; I was sure it was Arthur Mullard, the British actor famed in the 1970s for his roles in film and TV. Billy was certain that Mullard had died years ago, so most of our evening was spent debating whether we'd actually just seen the ghost of Arthur Mullard or not. The pre-*Google* and internet days, such fun eh? I read his obituary a couple of years later in the newspaper, and it turned out that old 'Arfur' had indeed lived out his final years in an Islington council house after his success, and spent much of his free time socialising in local pubs. I phoned Billy to call my bet in. Yus, my dear.

The essence and spirit of Paul Weller's outlook was best summarised and captured by the fact he sometimes covered jazz instrumental *Uhmm* by Bobby Hutcherson and Neil Young's *Ohio* in the same set. These may seem like unlikely bed-partners, but were the perfect mash-up for the times. I even got to meet Paul and Steve White for the first time on that initial tour, in Nottingham and Leicester, little knowing that I would go on to share a stage with them both almost thirty years later. Leicester had itself a bit of a reputation too, and we used to frequent the *Mosquito Coast* club nights every Thursday, where the resident DJ was a guy called Tony Minvielle, who played the best soul, jazz and rare groove in the area. Those nights were legendary, and Tony remains a friend to this day, continuing to champion new jazz and soul sounds via his regular show on *Jazz FM*. For a while, the city set the pace with its shops too, and *the Silver Arcade* had at least three or four independent outlets where I would never fail to get kitted out. Birmingham had a couple of top tailors, but for off-the-peg individuality, Leicester was the destination. Beads, tailored trousers, colourful knitwear, casual and cool, I found it one of the greatest periods for music and clothes. To complete the holy trinity, my beloved Leeds United won the Football League in '92. *Match of the Day* magazine voted Leeds supporters the best-dressed fans in the country, and I was proud to be the face of that style, pictured in the publication outside Elland Road before a home game. I was eating a bag of chips when they stopped me to ask if I minded having my photo taken for the magazine: not exactly the epitome of cool.

The Phoenix Festival, on our doorstep in Stratford-upon-Avon, replaced *Glastonbury* as the hip summer destination. Promoter Adrian Gibson had the foresight to mirror the times, curating a stage purely aimed at a soul, funk and jazz crowd, booking both heritage and contemporary artists. Imagine seeing the likes of Herbie Hancock, Jimmy Smith, Bootsy Collins, and early career performances from Jamiroquai, Cypress Hill, Mother Earth and Guru's Jazzmatazz project in a giant tent on an airfield in Long Marston! They even got the main stage headliners bang on too - over the course of the few years it was staged, I witnessed sets from Bob Dylan, Neil Young, Massive Attack, Bowie, the Sex Pistols, Parliament-Funkadelic, Van Morrison... it really was an incredible annual event, the right place at the right time. Bureaucratic red tape and local politics eventually shut it down, never to be resurrected. I still live in hope.

I had noticed a shift in the type of establishments where our own group could get gigs too. Polytechnics had become a thing of the past, and the Universities stopped booking bands such as ours, because dance culture was in vogue and had taken a hold, and it was far more cost-effective for them to book a DJ and put on a house or rave night than pay for a nine-piece touring band. The times they were a-changin'. Sometimes I'd experience first-hand the disparate nature of certain musical worlds, and the contrasts between them. One of the last few university gigs we did was up in Sheffield, where we were scheduled to play in a line-up that also included The Brand New Heavies and Roachford. We had played the hall up there on several occasions. The universities were always very well organised, with no expense spared when it came to the technical details, and logistics such as staging and sound. So on arrival this particular evening, we were somewhat surprised to see the humongous resident PA stack dismantled and shifted to one side, in favour of a tiny, makeshift system, with speakers the size of egg boxes flanking the stage. By now I knew the social secretary and booking agent of the campus fairly well, so I enquired as to what was going on, and why the PA had been replaced. Apparently, the headline act had insisted on using their own PA.

"What? Roachford prefers this set up to the in house rig?"

"Oh ... Roachford pulled out", replies Ann Marie, the ents officer.

"So who's responsible for this debacle?" I enquire. Ann Marie mumbles something, her hand over her mouth, it begins with S, that much I can make out.

"What? Who?"

" … Showaddywaddy ..."

OK, so not only have we now got a bunch of old sweats from a bygone era at the top of the bill, they also insist on using a PA system that looks like it was last used on the Waltzers at *Barker's Fun Fair* in 1975. On top of all this drama, they turn out to have egos the size of a small country. It really still is the '70s in their world. We are about twenty minutes into our set and their singer Dave Bartram is stood at the side of the stage, motioning at his watch. Alright Dave, keep your drape on...

Oddly enough, we went on to have further dealings with ex-members of '70s (s)hitmakers Showaddywaddy. Brian Harkins owned a venue in Nuneaton called *The Crazy Horse*, where Dance Stance regularly appeared. Brian was a lovely guy, always looked after us, and was devoid of any self-importance, unlike his former band-mates. He just had a burning passion for music, and was happy to give young bands starting out a leg-up or an opportunity to gig. Their drummer also owned a venue, which was situated out in the Leicestershire countryside, and was popular with bikers and females. It had itself a reputation, and in fairness, it was always busy, no matter what night of the week. I can only assume he was making a mint, as he would be more occupied with revving up his motorbike outside his club than being an amicable host. We only played his gaff once (although I'd been there on several occasions) and that experience was enough. We were treated like an inconvenience, even the sound engineer moaned most of the night because there were eight of us, and it meant he might actually have to do some work. The guy certainly thought he was doing us a favour by letting us grace his stage, and as soon as it became apparent to him that we were not a covers band or his standard fare, we were met with even more disdain. It seemed odd to me that a so-called professional musician who ran a live venue would pour scorn on a group of young lads trying to create and write music. I recall him lecturing me for about an hour on what I needed to do to be able to make it in "showbiz". Almost every sentence was punctuated with a reminder that he was a million-seller, pointing towards the gold discs adorning the walls of his office. Fuck me; anyone would have thought he was in the friggin' Beatles. It was all a power trip, kind of 'know your place, young man, I know this business' type of bollocks. The pinnacle of his disrespect came though when he tried to short us on the agreed fee for the night. Before I left, I doubled back and snuck into his office… I couldn't help but notice the kettle over in the corner… old habits die hard... I needed the toilet anyway. Enjoy your brew.

17 - JUST THE TICKET

I've been fairly fortunate over the years with my gig-going activities. Fortunate and dedicated. I'm kind of blessed to be of a certain age where I had the opportunity to catch some of the heavyweight artists and bands in their prime. I guess, ideally, I could have been a few years older, and have witnessed bands like The Wailers at their peak, or Marvin Gaye before he thought it was a good idea to do gigs in his underwear. I can't complain though, I have seen pretty much everyone I've wanted to, and though there's a few that were slightly past their sell-by date that I possibly wish I hadn't seen, circumstance has mainly conspired in my favour.

I have always been a regular attendee of concerts; I've been hooked from the moment I witnessed those skinheads and rude boys hurling themselves from the balcony at *De Montfort Hall* for the Madness matinee show at 12 years old (it was actually something of a disappointment and anti-climax to realise that this behaviour wasn't the norm at gigs). I got lucky with my job too, for as I have mentioned elsewhere, we were showered with free tickets to events via the record shop, in return for favours tickling the chart return machine and fudging sales figures on singles and albums. That opened up opportunities to see bands that I wouldn't necessarily have parted with my hard earned cash to see, and I was thankful for that, but more than often I would pay my own way. My disposable and non-disposable (... actually is money ever really disposable?) income went the way it still does to this day ... music, clothes, gigs (oh ... and of course through the turnstiles of either The Adders or Leeds United). Wherever possible I have retained all of my ticket stubs. I have books filled with them, which trigger some wonderful memories, the benefits I suppose of my hoarding nature; it's not all garbage you know. Flicking through those annuals documenting my nights out throughout the years, every page tells a story. The occasions that live longest in my thoughts are mainly those fortuitous occasions when serendipity reigned. I was never keen on guest-list gigs, I didn't trust them, always fearing that our names would be omitted from the list, despite countless assurances from the record label/promoter/artist or whoever was responsible for the invite.

To be honest it usually went according to plan, and I didn't encounter that many headaches or much hassle getting into venues, but on this one particular occasion our absence on the sheet of names proved to work in our favour. Hammy and I had taken a trip over to the *NEC* in Birmingham for a night out courtesy of *Warner Music* to see Echo & The Bunnymen. We arrived at the entrance and were ushered over to a kiosk where all of the names for the guest list were. The lady was very patient, and indulged us in every perceivable variation possible, from our names, to the shop's name, to the record company rep's name, nothing. We had been missed off, and of course, this was prior to the invention and use of mobile phones, so a simple phone call couldn't solve our issue. We dejectedly turned around and trudged off, not having sufficient funds between us to purchase a couple of tickets from the touts. Our luck was out, or so we thought. Just as we were waiting to cross a service road and make our way back over to the car park in disappointment, a van pulled up beside us, wound down its window and asked us if we had tickets for tonight's gig, and more to the point did we want to buy any? Mobile touts? They've spread their fucking wings somewhat, I thought. Hammy relays our plight to the two figures in the van, tells them we are pretty much potless, and are retreating back home in time for *Match of the Day*. After a brief conflab with one another, the man in the van and his mate inform us that they have *Access All Areas* passes for the arena. They have been contracted to rig up the staging and lighting, they have done their shift and are heading home. They decide there's not much point hanging about now in the vain attempt to make some money from their passes, so they take pity on us and hand over their laminate badges - "Get you anywhere these will lads, just don't say where you acquired them if you get pulled."

Me and Hammy are still sceptical, but do an about turn and head for the main entrance doors, where we are just ushered straight through.

"How far do you think we'll be able to get with these?" I ask Hammy.

"Let's fucking find out!" is the correct answer.

So we head down the concourse at the side of the *NEC* to the first checkpoint, which clearly states 'No unauthorised access beyond this point'. We flash our passes, and are immediately waved onwards. Then we walk across some steps, and arrive to the left-hand side of a dimly lit corner adjacent to the back of the stage. A security guy shines his torch in our path, we show him our *AAA* laminates, he simply pulls back a curtain and we find ourselves backstage at the *National*

Exhibition Centre. The clock has ticked on since our drama outside, and it's almost stage time for the Bunnymen. The support band have finished their set, and roadies scurry about, frantically moving equipment ahead of the main event. We do our best to stay anonymous. Impossible.

"What the fuck are you two doing here?" We turn to see a familiar face; it's one of the sound engineers that we know from our own gigs over in Coventry. He's here working for The Primitives, who have just come off stage as the opening act. We let on, but ask him not to. It's actually the perfect way to kill time while the lights are still up. We make ourselves appear important, but are mindful to blend in too, and I think our experience of hanging out backstage at gigs gives us an advantage for this hustle. I recognise another face in the vicinity "Alright Tony?" I say to a bemused-looking Tony Fletcher, who I recall from his days editing *Jamming* magazine and supporting The Jam with his group Apocalypse. Of course, he has no fucking clue who I am, but it makes me appear like someone at least.

Before Tony has time to quiz my identity, a door swings open and we find ourselves face to face with Ian McCulloch, Will Sergeant, Les Pattinson and Pete De Freitas. I can't help myself, and I slip into a role - "Have a good one lads, it's fucking heaving out there, twice the size of *Birmingham Odeon*, this lads." Now instead of looking at us like friggin' aliens and asking 'who the fuck are you?' Mac simply says 'cheers La', and tells us to help ourselves to a beer in the changing room if we want, as there's loads in there still. We soon clock the scene. The Bunnymen and their crew think we are the top boys at the venue, and the *NEC* venue crew think we are the top boys with the Bunnymen entourage. We must look the part, as no one thinks to examine our passes. We grab a beer, and help ourselves to the rest of The Bunnymen's rider too; sandwiches and snacks, then we take a walk up the ramp and plonk ourselves at the left wing of the stage for the duration of the gig. What an experience! It's the first time we had been privy to an arena concert of that magnitude at such close quarters (I could never in my wildest dreams imagine that I would be playing here on this very stage some thirty-one years later!). It's a huge step up for Echo & The Bunnymen too, and of course they rise to the occasion. Mac already believes his own legend and often claims that they are the best band in the world. Tonight they simply soared, and few could have argued that point. Only a few weeks after concluding the tour, Peter De

Freitas was tragically killed in a motorcycle accident, aged just twenty-seven. The Bunnymen never really recovered from such a massive loss.

For some reason we didn't think going to see NWA on their first tour of the UK would be a problem, and I'd never even considered that there might be racial tension hanging heavy in the air. It was never an issue or even a thought for me, I just wanted to go along because I loved their record and their antagonistic vibe, and I thought it would be a triumphant spectacle. It was the classic line up - Dre, Ren, Ice Cube, Eazy E and DJ Yella. Myself and Hammy were massive fans of hip hop and its culture, and of course we had long been fascinated with Black American music from Otis Redding to Frankie Knuckles, Hendrix to Bambaataa; it was our thing. So it was a real shocker for us to find ourselves surrounded with so much friction, a hostile atmosphere charged and cheer led by NWA member Eazy E, who was fuelled by rage and hate, and seemed a conflicted little dude. He whipped it up at the Hummingbird that night anyway, confrontational and uncompromising. I didn't mind it to be honest, in fact it was what I can only assume and imagine it would have been like to watch the Sex Pistols in their prime. The atmosphere was really heavy though, and turned menacing as the evening progressed. Somewhat unwisely perhaps, we decided to make a move out of the gig a few minutes early, just as NWA were finishing up their encore. We walked out into Dale End, and the streets were lined with gangs; the reputation of the occasion had heightened tension, and I suppose attracted opportunists too. Me and Hammy had only taken a few steps from the venue when we were approached from behind, and heard the demands for money. We kept on walking, doing our best to ignore the threats. I quickly glanced around just to gauge how close they were to us. It was a gang of about six to seven youths. I saw the vocal one of the posse drop his arm to his side, and could clearly make out the blade of a knife that he was concealing. I knew we had no chance if we attempted to run. My brain went into overdrive, trying to work a way out of this potentially threatening situation. Just then, fate played its card and intervened. Right bang on cue, a bus full of police pulls around the corner. Their very presence temporarily puts our predators on the back foot, and they begin to disperse. Fuck the Police? More like Thank Fuck for the Police!

The complimentary tickets from the record shop didn't always appeal to my tastes, but we'd pretty much go and see anything and anyone on the basis of it being something to do. What else is there to do on a wet Wednesday night? You might as well take up that offer of a ticket to see Chris Rea, he can't be THAT boring (he is). Ah, T'Pau? Go on then, it's something to do (so is trimming your toenails). I have seen some incredible gigs, but I've also seen my fair share of the banal and the preposterous. Punters who favoured heavy rock that frequented my shop always told me that I had never been to a proper gig until I'd seen Alice Cooper. In 1989, I got my opportunity, free tickets for his *Trash* tour. It was like a really bad pantomime, fake blood, the lot. These dudes obviously don't get out much. Depeche Mode? Fuck me, answers on a postcard, how depressing! I even saw Wet Wet Wet once for 'something to do'; what the fuck does he find so funny?

Once in a while though I would strike pure gold with the invites. No more so than when *Columbia Records* were trying their best to launch one of their American artists over here in the UK. They had set up a small regional tour, and were struggling to sell tickets. So, the *Sony* reps invited the local record shops to go along in the hope of procuring some favour there, maybe we'd take units of his new album and sales would grow organically, word of mouth. I was the only person interested from our bunch; we had five shops at the time (1994), and I couldn't get any of them to go with me. The main reason I wanted to check out this new kid on the block was because I was a big fan of his dad. I owned and pretty much loved all of Tim Buckley's records, and I particularly dug the ones no one else paid much attention to. *Blue Afternoon*, *Happy Sad* and the more avant-garde *Starsailor* got all the critical plaudits, but it was the lesser-known gems that really caught my ear, such as *Look At The Fool*, *Sefronia* and *Greetings from L.A.* Tim Buckley died of a drug overdose in 1975, and obviously I never got the opportunity to see him, so I was intrigued to find out if his son bore any musical resemblance. This was August '94, the actual week that *Grace* by Jeff Buckley was released in the UK. The venue was *Edwards No.*8, predominantly a rock club in the backstreets of Birmingham, and no-one was there. The only other faces I recognised were Mike and his mate from *Swordfish Records* in Brum. If I said there were sixty people in the audience, that still might be a generous estimation; let us just say it was sparse.

I grabbed myself a drink and pitched up at the front of stage, not knowing at all what to expect. I'd yet to hear or even see a picture of Jeff Buckley, and I'm only here because of who his dad is/was. The house lights go down and the band enter stage left. First thing I notice as soon as his figure is illuminated is that Jeff is strikingly good-looking. With chiselled, defined, handsome features, he looks like a less rugged version of his father. The resemblance is undeniable, and immediately, you sense Jeff Buckley's presence. I am reeled in already, and he hasn't even sung a fucking note yet. He doesn't speak, or take any cheap shot about the non-attendance. He doesn't even make eye-contact, he simply begins to sing, the band slowly, quietly filtering in behind his lead. My introduction to Jeff Buckley is a song called *Mojo Pin*, the opening track on his album *Grace*. There have only been a handful of occasions in my life when I have instantly realised that I'm witnessing something truly special and remarkable unfold in front of me. This was a game-changer. The kid was incredible, and I could immediately cease all the lazy father-and-son comparisons. Jeff Buckley was a superstar in his own right; he needed not his dad's reputation to prop him up. The gig was sensational, and I longed to call up everyone I knew that cared about music to hotfoot it over to this tiny space in a small corner of the country, where I was witnessing musical history being born a few feet away from my face. Take a moment to put this book down and search Jeff Buckley "*Mojo Pin* live at *Glastonbury* in 1995"; it should be there for you to see. Now imagine me, seeing exactly that as an opening number in a tiny club, where I am stood right in front of Jeff Buckley with only about another sixty folk for company. It was as outstandingly beautiful and as mind-blowing as I'm making out. The whole gig was. It's certainly one of the best and most unexpected nights of my gig-going experiences. The rest, as they say, is history.

I feel privileged to have been at the right place, right time for many gigs. It's difficult to pinpoint my favourite. Folk often ask me 'what's the best gig you have ever been to?', but I can't really give a definitive answer, as there have been so many memorable, momentous occasions that all mean so much to me for different reasons. The Jam at *Bingley Hall* and the rush of teenage kicks; Dexys unveiling *Don't Stand Me Down* on the *Coming To Tow*n tour; Tom Waits in Hammersmith Odeon; Prince, and the magnificent spectacle that was his *Lovesexy* tour in 1988, where he performed in the round at *Wembley Arena* (all three of Bananarama sat behind myself and Hammy, while Lloyd Cole perched beside us, complete with notebook and pen!); The Blue Nile at *the Town Hall* was emotional; Curtis Mayfield was sensational. I actually met Curtis prior to a performance outside the *Hummingbird* venue, and it was the only time in my life I was lost for words. I was literally verbally dumbstruck. We just smiled at each other, he said 'hello', and must have noticed that I was in a state of shock to casually bump into my musical hero in the street. He was actually pushing one of those scots-plaid shopping baskets, which probably added to my confusion.

Chuck Berry was an interesting one. I caught him in the early '90s, and I think I was about the youngest cat there. It was mainly full of quiffed-up pensioners catching a glimpse of a bona fide rocker, rolling out all their yesterdays. Chuck was fairly non-communicative throughout, he just ploughed on firing out hit after hit, occasionally fixing that wild-eyed glare upon his audience. It was obvious he was the real deal, a rock 'n' roll heavyweight, and even back then one of the last of his kind. I'd read up enough to be fully aware of Chuck's reputation and his sometimes erratic and unpredictable behaviour, so I took to the edge of my ringside seat as the set approached it's finale, and he invited members of the crowd to join him up on stage to dance along. Several couples clambered up to one side of the stage, where they merrily jived away with one another while Chuck remained a good distance away, centre stage, hollering out *Johnnie B. Goode*. It was all fairly civil and orderly for a while. Things soon got interesting when one of the punters, who was part of the congregation dancing to one side, decided he would walk over to Chuck Berry to shake his hand and embrace him ... Now, I'd read about this... it was Chuck Berry that told Keith Richards that in no uncertain terms, if a dude invades your space when you're performing, then you just gotta chop the motherfucker down; that space is your territory... I'd also actually seen footage of Keith putting this into action after a fan encroached onto the stage of a Stones gig in Virginia in the early '80s. So, I'm perched up on the balcony, stage left, and have the perfect view as this fella decides to make his way over in Chuck's direction. The first thought that raced into my mind was 'I wonder if he practices what he preaches?'

I honestly doubt that anyone else in that venue was anticipating it apart from me and Chuck, and certainly not the guy who was casually sauntering across the stage to pay respect to his hero. I fucking saw it coming. Chuck never even turned his head; he could obviously sense the geezer approaching. The split second I knew he was gonna get whacked was when I clocked Chuck's right hand drop to where the strap lock on his guitar was situated.... Sure enough, the instant the fella was in range ... BANG! He was sent crashing to the floor by a blow to the head with Chuck's cherry red *E 335 Gibson* guitar! Amongst the stunned silence that prevailed, I think I was a lone voice as I punched the air and proclaimed "Fucking have that, Rock 'n' Roll man!" I am sure I stood up too, and celebrated it like a *World Cup* winning goal. Not big, not clever I know, but fuck me, it was THE most Rock 'n' Roll moment I'd ever witnessed. In the immediate aftermath the guy remained laid flat out on the stage, the throng of jivers scurried sharply back to the safety of their seats, the audience gawped on motionless, jaws open wondering what the fuck had just happened, and Chuck Berry just slung his guitar back on and duck-walked off for another verse of *Johnnie B. Goode...*

18 - BOYS TO MEN

Somewhere along the way we grew up. Sort of.

Hammy and I both became fathers; he before me - his daughter Jasmine coming along in the February of 1988. I remember stepping off the train at Nuneaton after returning from a night of debauchery and wild abandon at *The Wag Club* in London Town, and heading straight to the hospital to see Hammy and Delisha, and to meet Jasmine for the first time. Staying in became the new going out for a while. Sure, we were still gigging and attending gigs, but many weekends would be spent sitting in the flat above the barbers, and letting Jasmine entertain us. Hammy and I were still fairly inseparable, a factor which possibly could have contributed to the eventual demise of his and Delisha's relationship. I'm not sure. For a while though, sunshine was in all of our lives.

A silly thing I always recall about jazz was sitting in front of *MTV* when she was about three years old. Nirvana were just blowing up and becoming huge, and she used to sing along to their hit *Smells like Teen Spirit*, but sing the words "and it's taters, yes it's taters ..." to the chorus. Our best mate and drummer Phil, of course, had the nickname Taters, because of his crisp-making ancestry (see Chapter 6).

Courtenay, Hammy and Delisha's son, came along four years later in the March of 1992. My own first-born son Mason was two years on from that, arriving in January 1994, and my life pretty much altered forever. I had responsibility. I wanted to be as great a parent as mine had been to me. I longed to make a success of it. I kind of fell at the first hurdle when me and Mason's mum, Celia, split up when he was only two years old. With the benefit of years of hindsight, it wasn't a failing at all; it was the right decision for both of us. We never really fell out, it just wasn't right for us to be in a relationship together, and we were sensible enough to face up to that fact early on. Celia is a great parent and soon found love, marriage and happiness elsewhere. Most importantly, Mason grew up in two loving homes as opposed to one. At first I viewed the breakdown of our family as a failure, but very quickly realised it was most certainly for the best, and it worked out to everyone's benefit.

Hammy was experiencing similar issues, and soon his relationship with Delisha had faltered and come to a natural end too. It was sad, but once again, soon enough it turned out to be for the best, and everyone went on to find happiness. Of course, even our future relationships weren't completely straightforward, and had a bizarre twist in their tales.

It was during the time I was doing my DJ-ing stints at *the Angel* that Hammy got together with Emma. Emma was part of an all-female ensemble that used to frequent gigs with our lot. They were a few years younger than we were, but would tag along to concerts with us, especially the funk and soul events. They were into clothes, music and having a laugh. We always looked out for them and made sure they were alright, that they were never hassled or taken advantage of. Our two social circles just gelled, and appreciated each other's tastes. They were a lot of fun, and I am sure they held our attitude and chivalry in the same high regard.

Hammy and Emma kind of segued together in the most natural, almost unspoken manner. They just started hanging out more and more, until soon enough they became an item. I was happy for them, as they were both happy. That's all you want for your friends, isn't it? Hammy had re-located across town into a flat inside the old Vicarage building, heading out towards Mancetter. It wasn't long before Emma moved in and they made it a home together. Emma had a sister a couple of years her junior, who was also part of their crew. I hadn't seen her for a while, as she had been spending time away at university, doing a fashion degree. She was effortlessly cool and very attractive, always smiling. I remembered her from way back, when I first saw her walking down Coleshill Road in *Adidas* green-stripe shell-toes (see chapter 16). Her name was/is Claire. Claire was back from university, and I would see her regularly, walking down my street to pick up her little sister Katie from school. Her grandad, Arthur, lived a few doors down from me too, so we'd stop, say hello and catch up once in a while. One day, I managed to pluck up the courage to invite her in for a cup of tea. We have now conversed over a cuppa for the last twenty-three years (and still counting). We got married, and now have two kids of our own.

But let's just rewind and jump back to the start for a moment...

The fact that Claire was Emma's sister was purely coincidental. I had fallen in love, and that was a very deep hole, one I didn't want to climb back out of. Once everyone had got past the "Oh, it'll never last" phase, we encountered one of the happiest and most fulfilling periods of our lives, two best friends who were closer than brothers, dating two sisters. We didn't plan it that way, it just happened. Not a single day passed by when the four of us didn't communicate with one another. If we weren't sitting around at one of our houses, out at a restaurant, or attending a gig, then we'd at least call each other up. The well of conversation never ran dry. It mattered not if we were on a weekend retreat away somewhere, or simply sitting in looking after the kids, laughter filled the air: simple pleasures and joyous times. And all of this while faced with such a delicate perspective on life. I wished for those wondrous days to last an eternity. The memories do, but of course, as Johnny Thunders once famously sang - *You can't put your arms around a memory.*

Yeah, there's something I haven't yet told you...

19 - ONE EYE IN THE SKY

2001, 9/11. One of those rare moments in life where everyone can instantly recall where they were, what they were doing, whom they were with. I was sat watching TV as the news broke, and live footage of the horrific events that unfolded that day beamed across the world. I was viewing it on television in Hammy's flat in the Old Vicarage. "Fuck me, Hammy, they're destroying America, this is fucking unreal, it's like a scene out of a film, it's surreal, the fucking Twin Towers have gone! Hammy... look, it's unreal, I can't believe what I'm watching ... Hammy look ... Hammy ..."

But Hammy couldn't look. Hammy couldn't answer or even make sense of what I was trying to tell him. I had momentarily forgotten. Hammy lay on the sofa next to me, fighting his own war. He could no longer take in what I was saying to him. His battle was very soon to be over.

Only several days earlier had the cancer spread and reached his brain. The change was almost instant, and the occasional incoherent rambling had now festered into the tragic state of a virtual inability to communicate. We would get fleeting moments, snatched conversations for maybe five or ten minutes, then he would slip back into semi-consciousness. I prayed for a miracle, but I knew in my heart this was the end.

We had been no more than kids when Hammy first complained to me about his knee – "Sheas, look at my legs, does one look bigger than the other to you? That knee looks bigger than the other and it hurts me sometimes ... what do you reckon Sheas?"

"Hammy" I replied, "You've got legs like fucking Ghandi, there's nothing on you man. Go to the doctors if it's hurting you, or if you're seriously bothered about it, see what they say".

The knee got mentioned every now and then, until it quite obviously became an issue. It stopped growing in proportion to the other, and started to give him a constant, nagging ache. Eventually it was diagnosed as cancer, at the start of 1992. The C-word freaked us out, but Hammy almost immediately faced it head-on. His outlook and approach, once he had digested the news, was one of complete positivity. What was happening was very, very real. He had no choice or option but to deal with it, and he certainly wasn't going out without a fight. And what a fight he put up too!

The treatment for his knee began with a course of radiotherapy, and so began our regular trips to the *Selly Oak Hospital* in Birmingham. I think I could still do that drive blindfolded, so often did we have to make that journey. From the off, Hammy was resolute, and mentally as strong as an ox. He treated those visits to the hospital, to deal with a life-threatening issue, the same as you or I would treat a trip to the dentist's, as an inconvenience, nothing more, and nothing less. In saying this, I must also hasten to add that neither was he in denial, or dismissive of his condition. He just simply got on with it.

One year later, at the turn of 1993, all started to look really positive. After the radiotherapy, he needed an operation on his leg, which initially seemed successful. The cancer had disappeared. He would now have to return every eight weeks, to monitor and check up on the situation. We all felt a great relief, and it appeared that my friend was out of the woods. Every second month we would drive over, and anxiously wait to be told that all was fine, to check in again in another eight weeks, then 'we will fully discharge you once we're 100% satisfied that all of the cancer cells have completely dispersed.'

It was I who felt like I was on my deathbed when I got the phone call. I'd caught chicken pox, ironically from Hammy's daughter Jasmine, and they hit me really hard. It brought a temperature so high that it was deemed to be dangerous, and I was delirious and hallucinating. The doctor was called, and I was ordered to take stone-cold baths to bring down the fever, and be put under a close watch. So there I was, a few days into recovering from all of this, feeling sorry for myself, when the phone rang. It was Hammy. I only ever heard him cry twice in his life, and this was the first time. I had never missed taking him to his hospital appointments, we always went together, and I always drove. Due to my illness, I couldn't make it this time, and he had to sort alternative arrangements (Hammy didn't drive). I knew that he wasn't keen on breaking tradition and having someone else take him - it was almost like a superstition, a ritual that we shared. From the very off that day, he didn't feel lucky. I came to the phone. "Fucking hell kid", he sobbed, "I've got it in my lungs and chest. I'm fucked, Sheas". My heart sank to the pit of my stomach. I felt helpless. We both cried. His battle again commenced, but this time the stakes were raised. This was the autumn of '93.

I visited him the next day, and he opened the door and straight away burst into fits of laughter, looking at my face, almost unrecognisable from the chicken pox – "Fuck me Sheas! You look like a cross between *the Elephant Man* and *the Singing Detective*. You look terrible!" That was him the very next day, more concerned about me, the tears had subsided and he'd already put the gloves back on – "What a pisser eh Sheas? We've just got to get on with it, mate".

And so, it began again... trip after trip to the hospital, chemotherapy, hair loss, operations... Quite early on into the process, they opened him up, picked out the tumours like a bunch of grapes, and wired him back up. Literally, he had mesh holding his rib cage together. Two days later, he'd be up and about, rolling joints. His smoking was never at any point brought into question, and he was always completely honest and open with the doctors and medical staff. Neither was he told or advised to curb it. He never smoked cigarettes, only cannabis. It became a part of his medicine, and he was certainly one of those rare souls that operated and functioned totally normally while under its influence. He didn't use it for any reason other than the fact that he enjoyed it. And it suited him.

By now Hammy had established a close relationship with his chief consultant Dr. Spooner, who had also succumbed to his characteristic charm. Spooner became fascinated by Paul's resilience and strength of character. The cancer would no sooner appear than it would disperse, and he would have months in remission. This pattern repeated itself time and time again for the next eight years. It mystified, but also delighted Spooner. Hammy's body just defied logic, and he lived almost a normal, balanced, untroubled life with the disease for a full nine years (almost two years with the knee, and just over seven years with lung cancer). Dr. Spooner simply instructed Hammy to carry on doing whatever he was doing, and that included his spectacular appetite for smoking dope.

The trips to the hospital were like six-month meal tickets, as every time they gave him the all clear, he knew he had another five to six months free of it until the next appointment date was due. If it was bad news, he'd just take a heavy sigh and a deep breath, and resign himself to the fact that he would have to spend a few days in hospital receiving more chemo treatment. I think I seemed more nervous than him in those waiting rooms. Once his name was called out, I would be shitting myself, and my heart would race until he reappeared with news. It got to the point where he could tell and forecast his condition by looking at his own X-rays. We would wait in one department for him to be X-rayed, then have to move on to another waiting room to see the doctor. Hammy without fail always opened up his file on the way to see the doctor to check his own X-rays. He became something of an expert himself. He'd certainly seen enough of them, so he knew exactly what to look for. He always knew before his consultation with the doc if he was riddled, or clear of tumours. Whatever the outcome, the ritual remained the same; he sparked a joint up once we returned to the car, and we usually stopped off at the *Selly Oak Tavern* for either a celebratory or a consolatory pint. In fact, we ended up having some good old days out on the hospital run.

It was sometimes easy to forget that Hammy had cancer. He was so upbeat, he still went out to gigs, meals, parties, and always dressed and turned out immaculately. He pretty much operated as normal, even when sometimes he would be feeling wiped out. His strength of character and his resolve were staggering, but (unfortunately) he wasn't *Superman*. His condition deteriorated just before the millennium. I remember buying him a book, and Hammy loved reading, but he couldn't get through it; the words weren't making sense to him, the lettering on the pages was just a jumble. We kind of knew then that he was slowly but surely approaching another stage. The millennium became a target. It wasn't really discussed, but I knew that he wanted to see the turn of the century. He was slipping, but he was determined. I have some photographs of the millennium New Year's Eve, and Hammy looks like a ghost. I was prepared for it there and then. As it happened, he once again improved, and miraculously once again picked up, and I started to think he was fucking invincible.

In his later years, I would honestly say that Hammy was as happy as I ever knew him. He was fiercely proud of his children, and had a great relationship with them. Our inner sanctum, and his home life with Emma were solid, and he enjoyed life. He had to. He had a unique perspective on it. The clock was ticking. His manner was always celebratory, he would plan nearly every second of my day, he was always up for an adventure, and of course, I was only too happy and grateful to be sharing them with him. It could be a trip up to the *John Smedley* factory in Matlock, where that day he bought every knit they had, in every colour. My car was so loaded and weighed down with *Smedley* jumpers that if he had lived to be a hundred years old he would never have found time to wear them all. Or, I recall the day we ventured over to the *Jewellery Quarter* in Birmingham to buy a gold watch. The money that mounted up while he was cocooned indoors ill would burn a hole in his pocket as soon as he was able to get out again. He took great delight in spending it while on a trip out. He was certainly on top form on those days. It was like a throwback to when we first met as kids. The exact same spirit prevailed.

The inevitable beckoned though. One final meeting was called with Dr. Spooner, and both Emma and myself accompanied Hammy. His condition had become irreversible. It was just a case of when, a matter of time. And that is exactly what Dr. Spooner had to tell us that day. Even Spooner was on the verge of tears. We got as far as *The Mailbox* in Birmingham City Centre, when Hammy told us to pull over for a minute. This would be the second time he cried, faced with a pending reality. The cancer had gone to his brain and there was no way back.

A few days after, I was sat on that sofa watching the world change forever on 9/11. Our own tower of strength finally came crashing down too. The 14th fell on a Friday, and that night we (Me, Claire and Emma) all left the flat for the first time in days, weeks even. One of us was always there with him, looking out, we never left his side. The *Macmillan* nurses would check in regularly and attend to his needs. They were fantastic throughout. It was suggested that maybe we took a break, step out for a while, even for an hour. The nurses would keep watch. It was a good idea. Claire and Emma went round to our house, while I took my good friends Neil and Scott's offer of popping over to Tamworth. They were also insistent I should get out, if only for a short while. It was the right thing for me to do, but my mind couldn't switch off from Hammy. I travelled back from Tamworth around 10 p.m. and joined the A5 at Stoneydelph. As I re-joined the road, down the junction and onto the dual carriageway, my car took on a life of its own, and span around, coming to rest facing in the opposite direction. Thankfully, there was no traffic approaching in my direction. In fact, the roads were deserted. I slowly turned the car around. Shaking and shook-up, I cautiously continued on my way down the A5 back into Atherstone. It was such a strange experience, like something else had taken over the operation of my car. It felt like a sudden power surge that I had no control over. Once I returned home, I didn't even get my first sentence finished to tell the girls of the bizarre event that had just occurred, when the telephone interrupted me. It was the nurse. She suggested that we should all return to the flat.

I knew it was over as soon as the phone had rung. At the flat, I opened the door to the bedroom, where he lay peacefully upon the bed, to see him for the final time. I said my goodbyes and that was that. We had no unfinished business, nothing was left unsaid and there were no regrets. Within that hour or so of us having left the flat, Hammy decided it was time to slip away. He was thirty-four years old.

I stood outside the Old Vicarage taking in the night air, composing myself and drying my tears in preparation to contact his nearest and dearest with the news. His dad, his mum, his sister, Delisha and the kids ... I was sick with sadness.

Of course, we knew everyone in town, even the funeral directors. It was our friend Eggy who knocked on the door to take his body away later that evening. Even he couldn't help but to be overcome with emotion, though he soon raised a smile – "Old Hammy, what a bloke..." then he proceeded to tell us a story about Hammy cutting his hair, that within moments had us all in tears of laughter (Hammy's advice to Eggy was that he had hair like fucking barbed wire, and that he should singe it all off and start again...)

And that sums Hammy up. He affected everyone who met him. He made an enduring, endearing impression. Everyone who knew him has a different story to tell about him, and in the days, weeks, months and years that followed it was nice to hear them. I used to say that he lived a life so full that he crammed into those thirty-four years what most people will never experience in seventy or eighty. He told me towards the end that he loved his life, and felt blessed that he'd had such a wonderful time. I took great solace in this knowledge, but as I look back today, it seems nothing but a tragedy. Life does go on, and life is a beautiful thing, never to be taken for granted. He had so, so much more to look forward to. I find it increasingly heart-breaking, as time passes.

Thirty-four is just far too young, especially for one who illuminated so many people's lives.

Emma, Claire and myself kind of muddled through the days after his death until the funeral. My dad's funeral thirteen years previously had just passed me by. I'd been numb, devoid of emotion, I couldn't even cry. The vicar said some words that could have been about anyone. I wasn't going to let that happen again. I decided I was going to stand up and speak myself. I'll forever be proud of doing that and making that choice. So too did Hammy's father, Paul Hanlon Snr. It's a big thing to take on, but it's certainly worthwhile overcoming any nerves and emotions, to be able to pay a proper, fitting and deserving tribute. Funny, that funeral turned out to be a cracking day, a true celebratory affair. That day didn't pass me by. I embraced it, and remembered him the way he would have wanted me to.

Hammy's spirit and lust for life will always be with me, as will our wonderful memories of countless, endless days and nights spent in each other's company. I truly felt lucky and privileged to know him so well. He taught me so much, simply by just being himself. Humble, gracious, honest, smart, thoughtful, loving, hilarious... he was all of these things and more: a gentle soul with the inner strength of a lion. He made me a better man, he filled me with belief and confidence, showed me how to be comfortable in my own skin, how to accept a compliment, how that to be interesting you must first be interested, and he most certainly showed me that the glass was, is and always will be half-full.

OUTRO...

Back at the beginning of 2011, myself and my wife Claire were staying overnight in London. We had travelled down to attend a book launch for a new publication on the Small Faces. Our friend Paolo Hewitt had invited us. Towards the end of the evening, Paolo said there was someone here I should meet, and whisked us off to be introduced to none other than Richard Barnes, author of what had become a style Bible to youths of our age, the *Mods!* book, first published back in 1979. We hit it off instantly, conversation and stories flowed, and it was a real pleasure to meet the man who was partly responsible for kick-starting my fascination with the modernist movement. His information was essential reading for kids such as I; it took us back to learn of the history that informed our future, an education.

We walked back to our hotel that night, from the East side of town over to the West, our spirits high. Claire had something on her mind. "You know Neil, it's such a shame that Hammy isn't here anymore to share nights like this. I was just thinking, out of all the people we know, he would probably be the only other person except for you that would have recognised that guy tonight, and it would have meant as much to him as it obviously does to you. It's heart-breaking really, there's so much more he could have seen and participated in." Hammy stayed on our minds and in our thoughts for the duration of our stroll. I shared her bittersweet sentiment.

Next day, instead of heading straight back up to the Midlands, we decided to have a look around the city, get some lunch and do a spot of shopping. Amongst other things we called in on a shop in Newburgh Street. This is situated right by Carnaby Street, so we decided to take a stroll down 'Memory Lane'. There's a photograph that I'm particularly fond of, one of Hammy and I stood outside *Melanddi's* as young mod kids at the start of the eighties. We are about fourteen in it. Claire and I find ourselves more or less stood in the same spot, so I ask her to get her camera out and take a picture of me stood in the same place as we were all those years ago, only with Hammy unfortunately missing. A 'now and then' thing for a keepsake, as it was fresh in our minds after the previous night's conversation. She took the photograph, and we carried on walking up Carnaby Street.

Not even one minute had passed (Claire hadn't even put the camera back in her bag), when my attention was drawn to a giant hoarding that was covering some construction work that was taking place. On it was a collage of large, blown up images celebrating Carnaby Street style. I looked up above my head at what was probably the most sizeable of all these images.

Staring back at us, waving and smiling, there he was – Hammy. It was a huge image of a photograph that I had been attempting to track down for several years. It was taken outside *Tiffany's* in Coventry in 1980. He was just thirteen. The picture was used in a magazine about the 2-Tone scene at the time. Claire and I stood motionless, silent, cold with goosebumps, a real moment. The timing was surreal. An amazing coincidence? Fate? A sign? Whatever, there he was, my best friend caught in an iconic moment in time, displayed for all to see on one of the world's most famous streets, one we used to frequent as kids. He would have loved that. The hoarding advertised a gallery a few streets away. I told them my story and showed them the image. Immediately, they found me the direct contact for the photographer who took the shot all those years ago, a lady by the name of Toni Tye. I subsequently wrote to her and again relayed my tale, and she was so kind that she sent a print of the photo for both myself and Hammy's children.

I carried on walking up Oxford Street with tears in my eyes, and I will remember that day for as long as I live. You can quite easily dismiss such occurrences as pure chance and fortuity, but it seemed no coincidence to me that very soon after this, quite literally months, my life started to get even weirder, beginning with John Bradbury walking into a North London pub and picking us out of obscurity to support The Specials on a two-month tour of arenas (Me and Hammy had been those teenage kids that the Specials message was aimed at, we attended the anti-racism gig at *The Butts* stadium in Coventry decades earlier). Then more recently our collaboration and subsequent friendship with Paul Weller (The very catalyst that started this journey, the reason we wanted to start a band as kids, the reason my mum's light got shattered when me and Hammy were miming to *Down in the Tube Station at Midnight* all those years ago). When all this unfolded, it was a lot for me to comprehend at first, beyond coincidence, beyond circumstance.
It's like we are chess pieces being re-positioned from above; at least that's the way I like to think of it. Before he passed, Hammy was fairly instrumental in making sure that I never gave up on my music, and

really encouraged me to continue with it all, even though he no longer could, due to his illness. He was around to see me start the fruition of what was to become Stone Foundation, he met and became friends with Neil Jones too. More than anyone, he was ecstatic that I had formed a completely new group at the age of thirty, and had decided to give it one more shot. He knew better than anyone that it was part of who I am, it was in my blood, it was my heartbeat.

As I began - by saying in my intro to this book - somehow, somewhere along the way anything and everything suddenly seemed possible. I've stood on the stage in front of thousands at *The Royal Albert Hall*, playing songs that I've written, looked to the side of stage and there's Paul Weller watching us, with Lynval Golding of The Specials. Backstage is Ronnie Wood, a real-life Rolling Stone. There's Roger Daltrey of The Who... Me? That kid from Atherstone... at *The Royal Albert Hall*? I look up to the balcony… *The Royal Albert Hall!* The crowd applaud, they cheer... I'm a part of this? Me? That kid from Atherstone?... I look up to the balcony. I think of my dad, I think of my mum... It's God's balcony I set my sights upon. I think of Hammy... his presence is always there. Somewhat ridiculously, all I can imagine while I am on stage at *The Royal Albert Hall* is being on stage at *Baddesley Youth club* thirty-plus years previously ... I think of Hammy and our wonderful days of innocence. *Boys Dreaming Soul*.

To be continued…

PLAYLIST – BOYS DREAMING SOUL

As I sat down to write this book, a soundtrack epitomising each and every chapter played out in my head. I was transported back to places, people and stories, just by thinking about the songs that we heard or played at the time. Not necessarily my favourite songs, but certainly tunes that echoed our steps. That's the real beauty of music for me, that a song can put you back in an exact moment, it has the power and ability to remind of who you were with, what you wore, who you were dating, what events were unfolding. I decided it would be a good reference if I shared a few tunes of those times with you. After all, these songs, and so much more, are the foundations of this book. Music ...it's…important...right?

Chapter 1 –

David Bowie - *Space Oddity*
T-Rex - *Telegram Sam*
The Beatles - *Strawberry Fields Forever*
The Kinks - *Come On Now*
Edison Lighthouse - *Love Grows (Where My Rosemary Goes)*
Don Farndon - *Indian Reservation*
The Rattles - *The Witch*
Clarence Carter - *Patches*
Wayne Gibson - *Under My Thumb*

Chapter 2 –

The Jam - *Tonight At Noon*
Squeeze - *Cool for Cats*
999 - *Emergency*
Devo - *Whip It*
Stiff Little Fingers - *Alternative Ulster*
Dead Kennedys - *California Uber Alles*
Zounds - *Can't Cheat Karma EP*
The Who *I'm One*
The Chords - *Something's Missing*
The Stranglers - *Nuclear Device*

Chapter 3 -

Dexys Midnight Runners - *There, There My Dear*
The Jam – *Start*
The Specials - *Do Nothing*
XTC - *Generals And Majors*
Undertones - *Tearproof*
Public Image Ltd - *Flowers Of Romance*
Linton Kwesi Johnson – *Inglan' Is A Bitch*
Teardrop Explodes - *Ha, Ha I'm Drowning*
Talking Heads - *I Zimbra*
The Prisoners - *Hurricane*
The Action - *The Place*
The Clash - *The Magnificent Seven*

Chapter 3b – Please see Chapter 3b

Chapter 4 –

Vernon Garrett - *Running Out*
Mel Williams - *Can It Be Me*
The Showstoppers - *Ain't Nothing But a Houseparty*
Felice Taylor - *I Can Feel Your Love*
Cliff Nobles & Co. - *Love Is All Right*
Gladys Knight And The Pips - *Ain't No Sun Since You've Been Gone*
Otis Redding - *Tell The Truth*
Diana Ross And The Supremes - *Back In My Arms Again*
Frankie Vali - *You're Ready Now*
Jimmy Radcliffe - *Long After Tonight Is All Over*

Chapter 5 –

The Style Council - *Long Hot Summer*
Booker Newberry III - *Love Town*
Freeez - *I.O.U.*
Haircut 100 - *Kingsize*
Blue Rondo A La Turk - *Klacto Vee Sedstein*
Spandau Ballet - *Chant no.1*
Aztec Camera - *Oblivious*
Orange Juice - *Rip It Up*
Gary Byrd And The GB experience - *The Crown*
The Who – *How Many Friends*

Chapter 6 –

I Level - *Minefield*
Working Week - *Venceremos*
Everything But The Girl - *Each and Every One*
The Kane Gang - *Closest Thing to Heaven*
The Redskins - *Keep On Keepin' On*
The Smiths - *William, It Was Really Nothing*
Lloyd Cole and the Commotions - *Are You Ready To Be Heartbroken?*
Elvis Costello - *Let Them All Talk*
Friends Again - *Lullaby no.2*

Steely Dan - *Peg*

Chapter 7 –

Sade - *Hang On To Your Love*
Graham Parker And The Rumour - *White Honey*
Nick Drake - *One Of These Things First*
Van Morrison - *Domino*
Joni Mitchell - *Edith And The Kingpin*
John Martyn - *Solid Air*
Tom Waits - *Big Black Mariah*
Martin Stephenson & the Daintees - *Coleen*
Prefab Sprout - *Bonny*

Chapter 8 –

Dexys Midnight Runners - *Until I Believe In My Soul*
Curtis Mayfield - *Freddie's Dead*
Prince - *Sign O' the Times*
Ian Dury And The Blockheads - *Sex & Drugs & Rock 'n' Roll*
Al Green - *Take Me To The River*
Maze *Joy And Pain*
Shalamar - *There It Is*
Marvin Gaye - *Flying High In The Friendly Sky*
The Doobie Brothers - *Minute By Minute*

Chapter 9 –

Spear Of Destiny - *All My Love*
The Valentine Brothers – *Money's Too Tight To Mention*
The Blow Monkeys - *Forbidden Fruit*
Animal Nightlife – *Mr. Solitaire*
Betty Wright - *Tonight Is The Night*
Graham Central Station - *Hair*

Chapter 10 –

Talk Talk - *Spirit Of Eden* LP
William De Vaughan - *Give The Little Man A Great Big Hand*
Edwin Starr - *Time*

Nolan Porter - *Keep On Keepin' On*
Robert Palmer - *Give Me An Inch*

Chapter 11 –

Peter Gabriel - *Games Without Frontiers*
Happy Mondays - *Kuff Dam*
Flowered Up - *Weekender*
Fela Kuti - *Expensive Shit*
Defunkt - *Illusion*
Ice T - *High Rollers*
Neneh Cherry - *Buffalo Stance*
S Express - *Theme From S Express*

Chapter 12 –

Jo Boxers - *Johnny Friendly*
Inner City - *Good Life*
Charles Wright & The Watts 103rd St Rhythm Band - *Express Yourself*
De La Soul - *Say No Go*
Young MC - *Bust A Move*
Soul II Soul - *Keep On Movin'*
Kate Bush - *This Woman's Work*
The Blue Nile - *Saturday Night*

Chapter 13 –

Chuck Brown And The Soul Searchers - *Bustin' Loose*
Bob Dylan - *Oh Mercy* LP
Van Morrison - *Coney Island*
Sinead O'Connor - *Mandinka*
Billy Fury - *Halfway To Paradise*
Chicago - *25 or 6 to 4*
The Pretty Things - *S.F. Sorrow Is Born*
The Stone Roses - *Fools Gold*
Lenny Kravitz - *Let Love Rule*
808 State - *Pacific State*
Joe Smooth - *Promised Land*
The Style Council - *Changing Of The Guard*

Chapter 14 –

Electric Light Orchestra - *Livin' Thing*
George Harrison - *All Things Must Pass*
The Beatles - *Something*
Tom Petty And The Heartbreakers - *Listen To Her Heart*
Roy Orbison - *She's A Mystery To Me*
Bob Dylan - *You're A Big Girl Now*

Chapter 15 –

The House Of Love - *Beatles And Stones*
Was (Not Was) - *Zazz Turned Blue*
T-Rex - *Hang Ups*
The Doors - *Peace Frog*
Tears For Fears - *Badman's Song*
Raze - *Break 4 Love*
Frankie Knuckles - *Tears*
Brother To Brother - *Chance With You*
Bottom & Company - *Gonna Find A True Love*
Sweet Charles - *Yes It's You*
Dave Pike Set - *Mathar*
Stevie Wonder - *I Wish*
Roy Ayers - *Running Away*

Chapter 16 –

Galliano - *Welcome To The Story*
Young Disciples - *As We Come (To Be)*
Omar - *There's Nothing Like This*
Gil Scott-Heron - *The Bottle*
Bobby Hutcherson - *Ummh*
Paul Weller - *Kosmos*
Crosby, Stills, Nash & Young - *Ohio*
Traffic - *Medicated Goo*
Maceo & All The King's Men - *Feeling Alright*
Guru - *No Time To Play*
Massive Attack - *Five Man Army*
Steve Miller Band - *Fly Like An Eagle*
Herbie Hancock - *Headhunters* LP

Chapter 17 –

Echo & the Bunnymen - *The Killing Moon*
Jeff Buckley – *Mojo Pin*
Prince – *Girls and Boys*
Chuck Berry – *Reelin' and Rockin'*
NWA – *Straight Outta Compton*

Chapter 18 –

Funkadelic - *Standing On the Verge of Getting It on*
Nirvana - *Smells like Teen Spirit*
Oasis - *Live Forever*
Sly And The Family Stone - *Family Affair*

Chapter 19 –

The Beta Band - *The House Song*
Van Morrison - *Summertime In England*
The Jam - *Boy About Town*
The Kinks - *Days*
Curtis Mayfield - *Move On Up*
Donny Hathaway - *He Ain't Heavy, He's My Brother*
Kevin Rowland - *The Greatest Love Of All*
Tim Hardin - *Satisfied Mind*

You may also enjoy these other book titles from *Days Like Tomorrow Books*

***Mojo Talkin'* and *Ignore Alien Orders* both include input from Neil Sheasby**

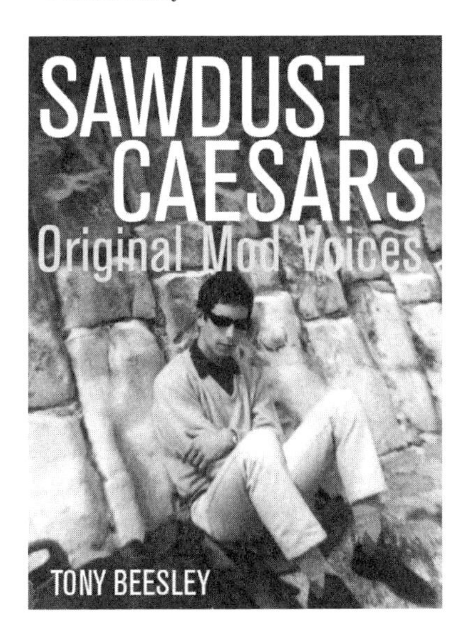

All titles available at www.tonybeesleymodworld.co.uk